100 Ways to Motivate Yourself

Revised Edition

Change Your Life Forever

100 Ways to Motivate Yourself

Revised Edition

Change Your Life Forever

Steve Chandler

CAREER
PRESS

Franklin Lakes, NJ

100 WAYS TO MOTIVATE YOURSELF
Cover design by Lu Rossman/Digi Dog Design
Edited by Robert M. Brink and Jodi Brandon
Typeset by Ellen S. Weitzenhofer
Printed in the U.S.A. by Book-mart Press

To order this title, please call toll-free 1-800-CAREER-1 (NJ and Canada: 201-848-0310) to order using VISA or Master Card, or for further information on books from Career Press.

CAREER
PRESS

The Career Press, Inc., 3 Tice Road, PO Box 687,
Franklin Lakes, NJ 07417
www.careerpress.com

Library of Congress Cataloging-in-Publication Data
ISBN 1-56414-775-4

To Kathryn Anne Chandler

Acknowledgments

To Robert Brink and Jodi Brandon for the masterful editing, to Lindsay Brady for the ongoing perception of success, to Stephanie Chandler for tirelessly working the cosmos, to Kathy for more than I can say, to Jim Brannigan for the representation, to Fred Knipe for the music on New Year's Eve, to Ron Fry for Career Press, to Karen Wolf for the international distribution, to Nathaniel Branden for the psychology, to Colin Wilson for the philosophy, to Arnold Schwarzenegger for a day to remember, to Rett Nichols for the tension plan, to Graham Walsh for the Tavern on the Green, to Terry Hill for the century's first real mystery novel, to Cindy Chandler for the salvation, to Ed and Jeanne for the Wrigley Mansion, to John Shade for the fire, to Scott Richardson for the ideas, to Ann Coulter for the wake-up calls, to Steven Forbes Hardison for coaching and friendship beyond the earthly norm, and to Dr. Deepak Chopra for unconcealing the creative intelligence that holds us all together.

And to the memory of Art Hill:
without whom,
no life, no nothin'.

Contents

Preface

Cyber Motivation

When this book was first written (in 1995), the entire world was not yet living in cyberspace. The Internet was a relatively new idea, and very few of us knew how big a part of our lives it would become.

As the new millennium dawned, a strange thing began to happen. People everywhere were writing again, just as people did in the 1800s when they took their quills out to write letters and diaries. The age of mind-numbing television viewing had been eclipsed by the age of chat rooms and e-mail.

This wonderful evolutionary jump in civilization gave this little book that you are holding in your hands right now brand-new life. All of a sudden the fight for limited shelf space in bookstores was not as important to a book's success. What became most important was the book's word-of-mouth "buzz" over the Internet.

Soon people were e-mailing other people about this book and the Internet bookstores (with infinite shelf space) were selling copies as fast as Career Press could print them. I began getting e-mails from readers as far away as Taiwan and Japan and as close as my computer screen.

When we leave this world, we will ask ourselves one question: What's different? What's different because I was here? And the answer to that question will be the difference that we made.

All of our thoughts and feelings won't matter any more when we are on our deathbeds asking that question. What will matter is the action we took and the difference that it made.

Yet we continue to obsess about our thoughts and become fascinated with our feelings. We are offended by other people. We want to prove we are right. We make other people wrong. We are disappointed in some people and resent others. It goes on and on and none of it will matter on that deathbed.

Action will be all that matters.

We could have made a difference every hour, every day, if we had wanted to.

So how do we do that? How do we motivate ourselves to get into action? How do we live a life of action and difference-making?

Aristotle knew the answer.

In the original preface to the original edition of this book, Aristotle gave the answer. The answer lies in motion. The answer lies in movement.

So what follows is the original snow angel preface to the original edition of the book. It's re-dedicated to everyone who has written to me about it:

When I was a child growing up in Michigan, we used to make angels in the snow.

We would find a fresh, untouched patch of snow and lie on our backs in it. Then, flapping our arms, we'd leave the impression of wings in the snow. We would then get up and admire our work. The two movements, lying down and flapping our arms, created the angel.

This memory of Michigan in the winter has come back to me a lot in recent weeks. It first happened when someone asked me what the connection was between self-motivation and self-creation.

While answering the question, I got a picture of snow. I had a vision that the whole universe was snow, and I could create myself any way I wanted by my movement. The movement of the actions I took would create the self I wanted to be.

Aristotle also knew how to create a self through movement.

He once said this: "Whatever we learn to do, we learn by actually doing it; men come to be builders, for instance, by building, and harp players by playing the harp. In the same way, by doing just acts we come to be just: By doing self-controlled acts, we come to be self-controlled; and by doing brave acts, we become brave."

This book contains 100 moves you can make in the snow.

> Steve Chandler
> Phoenix, Arizona
> January, 2001

Introduction

You Have No Personality

That each of us has a fixed personality is a myth. It is self-limiting and it denies us our power of continuous creation.

In our ongoing creation of who we are, nothing has a greater impact on that process than the choice we make between optimism and pessimism. There are no optimistic or pessimistic personalities; there are only single, individual choices for optimistic or pessimistic thoughts.

Charlie Chaplin once entered a "Charlie Chaplin Look-alike Contest" in Monte Carlo and the judges awarded him third place!

Personality is overrated. Who we are is up to us every moment.

The choices we make for our thinking either motivate us or they do not. And although clear visualization of a goal is a good first step, a joyfully motivated life demands more. To live the life you want to live, action is required. As Shakespeare said, "Action is eloquence." And as psychologist and author Dr. Nathaniel

Branden has written, "A goal without an action plan is a daydream."

Motion creates the self. In my experience as a teacher, consultant, and writer, I have accumulated 100 ways of thinking that lead directly to motivation. In my work as a corporate trainer and public seminar leader, I have often read and researched many volumes of a psychologist's or philosopher's work to find a *single sentence* that my seminar students can use. What I am always looking for are ways of thinking that energize the mind and get us going again.

So this is a book of ideas. My sole criterion in assembling these ideas was: How *useful* are they? I've drawn on the feedback I've gotten from my corporate and public seminar students to know which ideas make lasting impressions on people and which don't. The ones that do are in this book.

Since its first printing in 1996, this little book has enjoyed a success I never imagined. During its first five years of sales (sales that have continued to be strong every year, knock on wood) we have seen the emergence of the Internet as the world's primary source of information. People have not only been buying this book on the Internet, but they've been posting their reviews. What's wonderful about Internet bookstores is that they feature reviews by regular people, not just professional journalists who need to be witty, cynical, and clever to survive.

One such reviewer of *100 Ways* in its original edition was Bubba Spencer from Tennessee. He wrote:

"Not a real in-depth book with many complicated theories about how to improve your life. Mostly, just good tips to increase your motivation. A 'should read' if you want to improve any part of your life."

Bubba gave this book five stars, and I am more grateful to him than to any professional reviewer. He says I did what I set out to do.

"Making the simple complicated
is commonplace; making the
complicated simple, awesomely
simple, that's creativity."
—Charles Mingus,
legendary jazz musician

100 ways

1. Get on your deathbed

A number of years ago when I was working with psychotherapist Devers Branden, she put me through her "deathbed" exercise.

I was asked to clearly imagine myself lying on my own deathbed, and to fully realize the feelings connected with dying and saying good-bye. Then she asked me to mentally invite the people in my life who were important to me to visit my bedside, one at a time. As I visualized each friend and relative coming in to visit me, I had to speak to them out loud. I had to say to them what I wanted them to know as I was dying.

As I spoke to each person, I could feel my voice breaking. Somehow I couldn't help breaking down. My eyes were filled with tears. I experienced such a sense of loss. It was not my own life I was mourning; it was the love I was losing. To be more exact, it was a communication of love that had never been there.

During this difficult exercise, I really got to see how much I'd left out of my life. How many wonderful feelings I had about my children, for example, that I'd never explicitly expressed.

At the end of the exercise, I was an emotional mess. I had rarely cried that hard in my life. But when those emotions cleared, a wonderful thing happened. I was clear. I knew what was really important, and who really mattered to me. I understood for the first time what George Patton meant when he said, "Death can be more exciting than life."

From that day on I vowed not to leave anything to chance. I made up my mind never to leave anything unsaid. I wanted to live as if I might die any moment. The entire experience altered the way I've related to people ever since. And the great point of the exercise wasn't lost on me: We don't have to wait until we're actually near death to receive these benefits of being mortal. We can create the experience anytime we want.

A few years later when my mother lay dying in a hospital in Tucson, I rushed to her side to hold her hand and repeat to her all the love and gratitude I felt for who she had been for me. When she finally died, my grieving was very intense, but very short. In a matter of days I felt that everything great about my mother had entered into me and would live there as a loving spirit forever.

A year and a half before my father's death, I began to send him letters and poems about his contribution to my life. He lived his last months and died in the grip of chronic illness, so communicating and getting through to him in person wasn't always easy. But I always felt good that he had those letters and poems to read. Once he called me after I'd sent him a Father's Day poem, and he said, "Hey, I guess I wasn't such a bad father after all."

Poet William Blake warned us about keeping our thoughts locked up until we die. "When thought is closed in caves," he wrote, "then love will show its roots in deepest hell."

Pretending you aren't going to die is detrimental to your enjoyment of life. It is detrimental in the same way that it would be detrimental for a basketball player to pretend there was no end to the game he was playing. That player would reduce his intensity, adopt a lazy playing style, and, of course, end up not having any fun at all. Without an end, there is no game. Without being conscious of death, you can't be fully aware of the gift of life.

Yet many of us (including myself) keep pretending that our life's game will have no end. We keep planning to do great things some day when we feel like it. We assign our goals and dreams to that imaginary island in the sea that Denis Waitley calls "Someday Isle." We find ourselves saying, "Someday I'll do this," and "Someday I'll do that."

Confronting our own death doesn't have to wait until we run out of life. In fact, being able to vividly imagine our last hours on our deathbed creates a paradoxical sensation: the feeling of being born all over again—the first step to fearless self-motivation. "People living deeply," wrote poet and diarist Anaïs Nin, "have no fear of death."

And as Bob Dylan has sung, "He who is not busy being born is busy dying."

2. Stay hungry

Arnold Schwarzenegger was not famous yet in 1976 when he and I had lunch together at the Doubletree Inn in Tucson, Arizona. Not one person in the restaurant recognized him.

He was in town publicizing the movie *Stay Hungry*, a box-office disappointment he had just made with Jeff Bridges and Sally Field. I was a sports columnist for the *Tucson Citizen* at the time, and my assignment was to spend a full day, one-on-one, with Arnold and write a feature story about him for our newspaper's Sunday magazine.

I, too, had no idea who he was, or who he was going to become. I agreed to spend the day with him because I had to—it was an assignment. And although I took to it with an uninspired attitude, it was one I'd never forget.

Perhaps the most memorable part of that day with Schwarzenegger occurred when we took an hour for lunch. I had my reporter's notebook out and was asking questions for the story while we ate. At one point I casually asked him, "Now that you have retired from bodybuilding, what are you going to do next?"

And with a voice as calm as if he were telling me about some mundane travel plans, he said, "I'm going to be the number-one box-office star in all of Hollywood."

Mind you, this was not the slim, aerobic Arnold we know today. This man was pumped up and huge. And so for my own physical sense of well-being, I tried to appear to find his goal reasonable.

I tried not to show my shock and amusement at his plan. After all, his first attempt at movies didn't promise much. And his Austrian accent and awkward monstrous build didn't suggest instant acceptance by movie audiences. I finally managed to match his calm demeanor, and I asked him *just how* he planned to become Hollywood's top star.

"It's the same process I used in bodybuilding," he explained. "What you do is *create a vision* of who you want to be, and then live into that picture as if it were already true."

It sounded ridiculously simple. Too simple to mean anything. But I wrote it down. And I never forgot it.

I'll never forget the moment when some entertainment TV show was saying that box office receipts from his second *Terminator* movie had made him the most popular box office draw in the world. Was he psychic? Or was there something to his formula?

Over the years I've used Arnold's idea of creating a vision as a motivational tool. I've also elaborated on it in my corporate training seminars. I invite people to notice that Arnold said that you *create* a vision. He did not say that you wait until you *receive* a vision. You create one. In other words, you make it up.

A major part of living a life of self-motivation is having something to wake up for in the morning—something that you are "up to" in life so that you *will* stay hungry.

The vision can be created right now—better now than later. You can always change it if you want, but don't live a moment longer without one. Watch what being hungry to live that vision does to your ability to motivate yourself.

3. Tell yourself a true lie

I remember when my then-12-year-old daughter Margery participated in a school poetry reading in which all her classmates had to write a "lie poem" about how great they were.

They were supposed to make up untruths about themselves that made them sound unbelievably wonderful. I realized as I listened to the poems that the children were doing an unintended version of what Arnold did to clarify the picture of his future. By "lying" to themselves they were creating a vision of who they wanted to be.

It's noteworthy, too, that public schools are so out of touch with the motivational sources of individual achievement and personal success that in order to invite children to express big visions for themselves they have to invite the children to "lie." (As it was said in the movie *ET,* "How do you explain school to a higher intelligence?")

Most of us are unable to see the truth of who we could be. My daughter's school developed an unintended solution to that difficulty: If it's hard for you to imagine the potential in yourself, then you might want to begin by expressing it as a fantasy, as did the children who wrote the poems. Think up some stories about who you would like to be. Your subconscious mind doesn't know you're fantasizing (it either receives pictures or doesn't).

Soon you will begin to create the necessary blueprint for stretching your accomplishments. Without a picture of your highest self, you can't live into that self. Fake it till you make it. The lie will become the truth.

4. Keep your eyes on the prize

Most of us never really focus. We constantly feel a kind of irritating psychic chaos because we keep trying to think of too many things at once. There's always too much up there on the screen.

There was an interesting motivational talk on this subject given by former Dallas Cowboys coach Jimmy Johnson to his football players before the 1993 Super Bowl:

"I told them that if I laid a two-by-four across the room, everybody there would walk across it and not fall, because our focus would be that we were going to walk that two-by-four, But if I put that same two-by-four 10 stories high between two buildings only a few would make it, because the focus would be on falling. Focus is everything. The team that is more focused today is the team that will win this game."

Johnson told his team not to be distracted by the crowd, the media, or the possibility of losing, but to focus on each play of the game itself just as if it were a good practice session.

The Cowboys won the game 52-17.

There's a point to that story that goes way beyond football. Most of us tend to lose our focus in life because we're perpetually worried about so many negative possibilities. Rather than focusing on the two-by-four, we worry about all the ramifications of falling. Rather than focusing on our goals, we are distracted by our worries and fears.

But when you focus on what you want, it will come into your life. When you focus on being a happy and motivated person, that is who you will be.

5. Learn to sweat in peace

The harder you are on yourself, the easier life is on you. Or, as they say in the Navy Seals, the more you sweat in peacetime, the less you bleed in war.

My childhood friend Rett Nichols was the first to show me this principle in action. When we were playing Little League baseball, we were always troubled by how fast the pitchers threw the ball. We were in an especially good league, and the overgrown opposing pitchers, whose birth certificates we were always demanding to see, fired the ball in to us at alarming speeds during the games.

We began dreading going up to the plate to hit. It wasn't fun. Batting had become something we just tried to get through without embarrassing ourselves too much.

Then Rett got an idea.

"What if the pitches we faced in games were slower than the ones we face every day in practice?" Rett asked.

"That's just the problem," I said. "We don't know anybody who can pitch that fast to us. That's why, in the games, it's so hard. The ball looks like an aspirin pill coming in at 200 miles an hour."

"I know we don't know anyone who can throw a baseball that fast," said Rett. "But what if it wasn't a baseball?"

"I don't know what you mean," I said.

Just then Rett pulled from his pocket a little plastic golf ball with holes in it. The kind our dads used to hit in the backyard for golf practice.

"Get a bat," Rett said.

I picked up a baseball bat and we walked out to the park near Rett's house. Rett went to the pitcher's mound but came in about three feet closer than usual. As I stood at the plate, he fired the little golf ball past me as I tried to swing at it.

"Ha ha!" Rett shouted. "That's faster than *anybody* you'll face in little league! Let's get going!"

We then took turns pitching to each other with this bizarre little ball humming in at incredible speeds. The little plastic ball was not only hilariously fast, but it curved and dropped more sharply than any little leaguer's pitch could do.

By the time Rett and I played our next league game, we were ready. The pitches looked like they were coming in slow motion. Big white balloons.

I hit the first and only home run I ever hit after one of Rett's sessions. It was off a left-hander whose pitch seemed to hang in the air forever before I creamed it.

The lesson Rett taught me was one I've never forgotten. Whenever I'm afraid of something coming up, I will find a way to do something that's even harder or scarier. Once I do the harder thing, the real thing becomes fun.

The great boxer Muhammad Ali used to use this principle in choosing his sparring partners. He'd make sure that the sparring partners he worked with before a fight were *better* than the boxer he was going up against in the real fight. They might not always be better all-around, but he found sparring partners who were each better in one certain way or another than his upcoming opponent. After facing them, he knew going into each fight that he had already fought those skills and won.

You can always "stage" a bigger battle than the one you have to face. If you have to make a presentation in front of someone who scares you, you can always rehearse it first in front of someone who scares you more. If you've got something hard to do and you're hesitant to do it, pick out something even harder and do that first.

Watch what it does to your motivation going into the "real" challenge.

6. Simplify your life

The great Green Bay Packer's football coach Vince Lombardi was once asked why his world championship team, which had so many multi-talented players, ran such a simple set of plays. "It's hard to be aggressive when you're confused," he said.

One of the benefits of creatively planning your life is that it allows you to simplify. You can weed out, delegate, and eliminate all activities that don't contribute to your projected goals.

Another effective way to simplify your life is to combine your tasks. Combining allows you to achieve two or more objectives at once.

For example, as I plan my day today, I notice that I need to shop for my family after work. That's a task I can't avoid because we're running out of everything. I also note that one of my goals is to finish reading my daughter Stephanie's book reports. I realize, too, that I've made a decision to spend more time doing things with all my kids, as I've tended lately to just come home and crash at the end of a long day.

An aggressive orientation to the day—making each day simpler and stronger than the day before—allows you to look at all of these tasks and small goals and ask yourself, "What can I combine?" (Creativity is really little more than making unexpected combinations, in music, architecture, anything, including your day.)

After some thought, I realize that I can combine shopping with doing something with my children. (That looks obvious and easy, but I can't count the times I mindlessly go shopping, or do things on my own just to get them done, and then run out of time to play with the kids.)

I also think a little further and remember that the grocery store where we shop has a little deli with tables in it. My kids love to make lists and go up and down the aisles themselves to fill the grocery cart, so I decide to read my daughter's book reports at the deli while they travel the aisles for food. They see where I'm sitting, and keep coming over to update me on what they are choosing. After an hour or so, three things have happened at once: 1) I've done something with the kids; 2) I've read through the book reports; and 3) the shopping has been completed.

In her book, *Brain Building*, Marilyn Vos Savant recommends something similar to simplify life. She advises that we make a list of absolutely every small task that has to be done, say, over the weekend, and then do them all at once, in one exciting focused action. A manic blitz. In other words, fuse all small tasks together and make the doing of them one task so that the rest of the weekend is absolutely free to create as we wish.

Bob Koether, who I will talk about later as the president of Infincom, has the most simplified time management system I've ever seen in my life. His method is this: Do everything right on the spot—don't put anything unnecessarily into your future. Do it now, so that the future is always wide open. Watching him in action is always an experience.

I'll be sitting in his office and I'll mention the name of a person whose company I'd like to take my training to in the future.

"Will you make a note to get in touch with him and let him know I'll be calling?" I ask.

"Make a *note?*" he asks in horror.

The next thing I know, before I can say anything, Bob's wheeling in his chair and dialing the person on the phone. Within two minutes he's scheduled a meeting between the person and me and after he puts down the phone he says, "Okay, done! What's next?"

I tell him I've prepared the report he wanted on training for his service teams and I hand it to him.

"You can read it later and get back to me," I offer.

"Hold on a second," he says, already deeply absorbed in reading the report's content. After 10 minutes or so, during which time he's read much of what interests him aloud, the report has been digested, discussed, and filed.

It's a time management system like no other. What could you call it? Perhaps, Handle Everything Immediately. It keeps Bob's life simple. He is an aggressive and successful CEO, and, as Vince Lombardi said, "It's hard to be aggressive when you're confused."

Most people are reluctant to see themselves as being creative because they associate creativity with complexity. But creativity is simplicity.

Michelangelo said that he could actually *see* his masterpiece, "The David," in the huge, rough rock he discovered in a marble quarry. His only job, he said, was to carve away what wasn't necessary and he would have his statue. Achieving simplicity in our cluttered and hectic lives is also an ongoing process of carving away what's not necessary.

My most dramatic experience of the power of simplicity occurred in 1984 when I was hired to help write the television and radio advertisements for Jim Kolbe, a candidate for United States Congress running in Arizona's Fifth District. In that campaign, I saw first-hand how focus, purpose, and simplicity can work together to create a great result.

Based on prior political history, Kolbe had about a 3 percent chance of winning the election. His opponent was a popular incumbent congressman, during a time when incumbents were almost never defeated by challengers. In addition, Kolbe was a Republican in a largely Democratic district. And the final strike against him was that he had tried once before to defeat this same man, Jim McNulty, and had lost. The voters had already spoken on the issue.

Kolbe himself supplied the campaign with its sense of purpose. A tireless campaigner with unwavering principles, he emanated his sense of mission and we all drew energy from him.

Political consultant Joe Shumate, one of the shrewdest people I've ever worked with, kept us all focused with consistent campaign strategy. It was the job of the advertising and media work to keep it strong and simple.

Although our opponent ran nearly 15 different TV ads, each one about a different issue, we determined from the outset that we would stick to the same message throughout, from the first ad to the last. We basically ran the same ad over and over. We knew that although the district was largely Democratic, our polling showed that philosophically it was more conservative. Kolbe himself was conservative, so his views coincided with the voters' better than our opponent's did, although the voters weren't yet aware of it. By having each of our ads focused on our simple theme—who better represents *you*—we gained rapidly in the polls as election night neared.

The nightlong celebration of Jim Kolbe's upset victory brought a huge message home to me: The simpler you keep it, the stronger it gets. Kolbe won a close victory that night, but he remains in Congress today, more than 10 years later, and his victory margins are now huge. He has never complicated his message, and he has kept his politics strong and simple, even when it looked unpopular to do so.

It's hard to stay motivated when you're confused. When you simplify your life, it gathers focus. The more you can focus your life, the more motivated it gets.

7. Look for the lost gold

When I am happy, I see the happiness in others. When I am compassionate, I see the compassion in other people. When I am full of energy and hope, I see opportunities all around me.

But when I am angry, I see other people as unnecessarily testy. When I am depressed, I notice that people's eyes look sad. When I am weary, I see the world as boring and unattractive.

Who I am is what I see!

If I drive into Phoenix and complain, "What a crowded, smog-ridden mess this place is!" I am really expressing what a crowded, smog-ridden mess *I* am at that moment. If I had been feeling motivated that day, and full of hope and happiness, I could just as easily have said, while driving into Phoenix, "Wow, what a thriving, energetic metropolis this is!" Again, I would have been describing my inner landscape, not Phoenix's.

Our self-motivation suffers most from how we choose to see the circumstances in our lives. That's because we don't see things as they are, we see things as *we* are.

In every circumstance, we can look for the gold, or look for the filth. And what we look for, we find. The best starting point for self-motivation is in what we choose to look for in what we see around us. Do we see the opportunity everywhere?

"When I open my eyes in the morning," said Colin Wilson, "I am not confronted by the world, but by a million possible worlds."

It is always our choice. Which world do we want to see today? Opportunity is life's gold. It's all you need to be happy. It's the fertile field in which you grow as a person. And opportunities are like those subatomic quantum particles that come into existence only when they are seen by an observer. Your opportunities will multiply when you choose to see them.

8. Push all your own buttons

Have you ever peeked into the cockpit of a large airliner as you boarded a plane? It's an impressive display of buttons, levers, dials, and switches under one big windshield.

What if, as you were boarding, you overheard the pilot say to the co-pilot, "Joe, remind me, what does this set of buttons do?"

If I heard that, it would make it a rough flight for me. But most of us pilot our own lives that way, without much knowledge of the instruments. We don't take the time to learn where our own buttons are, or what they can do.

From now on, make it a personal commitment to notice everything that pushes your buttons. Make a note of everything that inspires you. That's your control panel. Those buttons operate your whole system of personal motivation.

Motivation doesn't have to be accidental. For example, you don't have to wait for hours until a certain song comes on the radio that picks up your spirits. You can control what songs you hear.

If there are certain songs that always lift you up, make a tape or CD of those songs and have it ready to play in your car. Go through all of your music and create a "greatest motivational hits" tape for yourself.

Use the movies, too.

How many times do you leave a movie feeling inspired and ready to take on the world? Whenever that happens, put the name of the movie in a special notebook that you might label "the right buttons." Six months to a year later, you can rent the movie and get the same inspired feeling. Most movies that inspire us are even better the second time around.

You have much more control over your environment than you realize. You can begin programming yourself consciously to be more and more focused and motivated. Get to know your control panel and learn how to push your own buttons. The more you know about how you operate, the easier it will be to motivate yourself.

9. Build a track record

It's not what we *do* that makes us tired—it's what we don't do. The tasks we *don't* complete cause the most fatigue.

I was giving a motivational seminar to a utility company recently, and during one of the breaks a small man who looked to be in his 60s came up to me.

"My problem," he said, "is that I never seem to finish anything. I'm always starting things—this project and that, but I never finish. I'm always off on to something else before anything is completed."

He then asked whether I could give him some affirmations that might alter his belief system. He correctly saw the problem as being one of belief. Because he did not believe he was a good finisher, he did not finish anything. So he wanted a magical word or phrase to repeat to himself that would brainwash him into being different.

"Do you think affirmations are what you need?" I asked him. "If you had to learn how to use a computer, could you do it by sitting on your bed and repeating the affirmations, 'I know how to use a computer. I am great at using computers. I am a wizard on a computer'?"

He admitted that affirmations would probably have no effect on his ability to use a computer.

"The best way to change your belief system is to change the *truth* about you," I said. "We believe the truth faster than we believe false affirmations. To believe that you are a good finisher, you must begin by building a track record of finished tasks."

He followed my suggestions with great enthusiasm. He bought a notebook and at the top of the first page he wrote, "Things I've Finished." Each day, he made a point of setting small goals and finishing them. Whereas in the past he would be sweeping his front walk and leave it unfinished when the phone rang, now he'd let the phone ring so he could finish the job and record it in his notebook. The more things he wrote down, the more confident he became that he was truly becoming a finisher. And he had a notebook to prove it.

Consider how much more permanent his new belief was than if he had tried to do it with affirmations. He could have whispered to himself all night long, "I am a great finisher," but the right side of his brain would have known better. It would have said to him, "No you're not."

Stop worrying about what you think of yourself and start building a track record that proves that you can motivate yourself to do whatever you want to do.

10. Welcome the unexpected

Most people do not see themselves as being creative, but we all are. Most people say, "My sister's creative, she paints," or "My father's creative, he sings and writes music." We miss the point that we are *all* creative.

One of the reasons we don't see ourselves that way is that we normally associate being "creative" with being "original." But in reality, creativity has nothing to do with originality—it has everything to do with being *unexpected*.

You don't have to be original to be creative. In fact, it sometimes helps to realize that no one is original.

Even Mozart said that he never wrote an original melody in his life. His melodies were all recombinations of old folk melodies.

Look at Elvis Presley. People thought he was a true original when he first came upon the scene. But he wasn't. He was just the first white person to ever sing with enthusiasm. His versions of songs, however, were often direct copies from African-American rhythm and blues singers. Elvis acknowledged that his entire style was a combination of Little Richard, Jackie Wilson, and James Brown, as well as a variety of gospel singers.

Although Elvis wasn't original, he *was* creative. Because he was so unexpected.

If you believe you were created in the image of your Creator, then you must, therefore, be creative. Then, if you're willing to *see yourself* as creative, you can begin to cultivate it in everything you do. You can start coming up with all kinds of unexpected solutions to the challenges that life throws at you.

11. Find your master key

I used to have the feeling that everyone else in life had at one time or another been issued instruction books on how to make life work. And I, for some reason, wasn't there when they passed them out.

I felt a little like the Spanish poet Cesar Vallejo, who wrote, "Well, on the day I was born, God was sick."

Still struggling in my mid-30s with a pessimistic outlook and no sense of purpose, I voiced my frustration once to a friend of mine, Dr. Mike Killebrew, who recommended a book to me. Until that time, I didn't really believe that there could be a book that could tell you how to make your life work.

The name of the book was *The Master Key to Riches* by Napoleon Hill. It sat on my shelf for quite awhile. I didn't believe in motivational books or self-help. They were for weak and gullible fools. I was finally persuaded to read the book by the word *riches* in the title. Riches would be a welcome addition to my life. Riches were probably what I needed to make me happy and wipe out my troubles.

What the book actually did was a lot more than increase my earning capacity (although by practicing the principles in the book, my earnings doubled in less than a year). Napoleon Hill's advice ultimately sparked a fire in me that changed my entire life.

I soon acquired an ability that I would later realize was self-motivation. After reading that book, I read all of Napoleon Hill's books. I also began buying motivational audiobooks for listening to in my car and for playing by my bed as I went to sleep each night. Everything I had learned in school, in college, and from my family and friends was out the window. Without fully understanding it, I was engaging in the process of completely rebuilding my own thinking. I was, thought by thought, replacing the old cynical and passive orientation to life with a new optimistic and energetic outlook.

So, what is this master key to riches?

"The great master key to riches," said Hill, "is nothing more or less than the self-discipline necessary to help you take full and complete possession of your own mind. Remember, it is profoundly significant that the only thing over which you have complete control is your own mental attitude."

Taking complete possession of my own mind would be a lifelong adventure, but it was one that I was excited about beginning.

Maybe Hill's book will not be your own master key, but I promise you that you'll find an instruction book on how to make your life work if you keep looking. It might be *The Power of Now* by Eckhart Tolle, *The Last Word in Power* by Tracy Goss, *Frankenstein's Castle* by Colin Wilson, or *The Six Pillars of Self-Esteem* by Nathaniel Branden. All those books would have worked the primary transformation for me, and they have all taken me higher up the motivational ladder. Your own key might even come from the spiritual literature of your choice. You'll find it when you're ready to seek. It's out there waiting for you.

12. Put your library on wheels

One of the greatest opportunities for motivating yourself today lies in the way you use your drive time.

There is no longer any excuse for time in the car to be downtime or frustrating or time that isn't motivating. With the huge variety of audiotapes and CDs now available, you can use your time on the road to educate and motivate yourself at the same time.

When we use our time in the car to simply listen to hip-hop or to curse traffic, we are undermining our own frame of mind. Moreover, by listening to tabloid-type "news" programs for too long a period of time, we actually get a distorted view of life. News programs today have one goal: to shock or sadden the listener. The most vulgar and horrific stories around the state and nation are searched for and found.

I experienced this firsthand when I worked for a daily newspaper. I saw how panicked the city desk got if there were no murders or rapes that day. I watched as they tore through the wire stories to see if a news item from another state could be gruesome enough to save the front page. If there's no drowning, they'll reluctantly go with a near-drowning.

There is nothing wrong with this. It's not immoral or unethical. It feeds the public's hunger for bad news. It's exactly what people want, so, in a way, it is a service.

But it reaches its most damaging proportions when the average listener to a car radio believes that all this bad news is a true and fair reflection of what's happening in the world. It's not. It is deliberately selected to spice up the broadcast and keep people listening. It is designed to horrify, because horrified people are a riveted audience and advertisers like it that way.

The media have also found ways to extend the stories that are truly horrible, so that we don't hear them just once. If a plane goes down, we can listen all week long as investigators pick through the wreckage and family members weep before the microphones. A week later, playing the last words of the pilots found in the black box, on the air, extends the story further.

In the meantime, while we are glued to our news stations, air safety is better than ever before. Literally millions of planes are taking off and landing without incident. Deaths per passenger mile are decreasing every year as the technology for safe flight improves. But is that news? No. And because my seminar schedule requires that I travel a lot by air, I can see up close what the so-called "news" has done to our psyches. Simple turbulence in the air will cause my fellow passengers' eyes to enlarge and their hands to grip their armrests in terror. The negative programming of our minds has had a huge impact on us.

If we would be more selective with how we program our minds while we are driving, we could have some exciting breakthroughs in two important areas: knowledge and motivation. There are now hundreds of audiobook series on self-motivation, on how to use the Internet, on health, on goal setting, and on all the useful subjects that we need to think about if we're going to grow.

As Emerson once said, "We become what we think about all day long." (I first heard that sentence, years ago, while driving in my car listening to an Earl Nightingale audio program!) If we leave what we think about to chance, or to a tabloid radio station, then we lose a large measure of control over our own minds.

Many people today drive a great deal of the time. With motivational and educational audiobooks, it has been estimated that drivers can receive the equivalent of a full semester in college with three months' worth of driving. Most libraries have large sections devoted to audiobooks, and all the best and all the current audiobooks are now available on Internet bookseller's sites.

Are all motivational programs effective? No. Some might not move you at all. That's why it's good to read the customer reviews before buying an audio program over the Internet.

But there have been so many times when a great motivational audio played in my car has had a positive impact on my frame of mind and my ability to live and work with enthusiasm.

One moment stands out in my memory above all others, although there have been hundreds. I was driving in my car one day listening to Wayne Dyer's classic audio series, *Choosing Your Own Greatness*. At the end of a long, moving argument for not making our happiness dependent on some material object hanging out there in our future, Dyer said, "There is no way to happiness. Happiness is the way."

That one thought eased itself into my mind at that moment and never left it. It is not an "original" thought, but Dyer's gentle presentation, so filled with serene joy and so effortlessly spoken, changed me in a way that no ancient volume of wisdom ever could have. That's one of the powers of the audiobook form of learning: It simulates an extremely intimate one-on-one experience.

Wayne Dyer, Marianne Williamson, Caroline Myss, Barbara Sher, Tom Peters, Nathaniel Branden, Earl Nightingale, Alan Watts, and Anthony Robbins are just a few motivators whose tapes have changed my life. You'll find your own favorites.

You don't have to find time to go read at the library. Forget the library. You are already driving in one.

13. Definitely plan your work

Some of us may think we're too depressed right now to start on a new course of personal motivation. Or we're too angry. Or we're too upset about certain problems.

But Napoleon Hill insisted that that's the perfect time to learn one of life's most unusual rules: "There is one unbeatable rule for the mastery of sorrows and disappointments, and that is the transmutation of those emotional frustrations through definitely planned work. It is a rule which has no equal."

Once we get the picture of who we want to be, "definitely planned work" is the next step on the path. Definitely planned work inspires the energy of purpose. Without it, we suffer from a weird kind of intention deficit disorder. We're short on intention. We don't know where we're going or what we're up to.

When I was a training instructor at a time-management company many years ago, we taught people in business how to maximize time spent on the job. The primary idea was this: One hour of planning saves three hours of execution.

However, most of us don't feel we have time for that hour of planning. We're too busy cleaning up yesterday's problems (that were caused by lack of planning). We don't yet see that planning would be the most productive hour we spend. Instead, we wander unconsciously into the workplace and react to crises. (Again, most of which result from a failure to plan.)

A carefully planned meeting can take a third of the time that an unplanned free-for-all takes. A carefully planned day can take a third of the time that an unplanned free-for-all day takes.

My friend Kirk Nelson manages a large sales staff at a major radio station. His success in life was moderate until he discovered the principle of definitely planned work. Now he spends two hours each weekend on his computer planning the week ahead.

"It's made all the difference in the world," he said. "Not only do I get three times the work done, but I feel so in control. The week feels like my week. The work feels like my work. My life feels like my life."

It is impossible to work with a definite sense of purpose and be depressed at the same time. Carefully planned work will motivate you to do more and worry less.

14. Bounce your thoughts

If you've ever coached or worked with kids who play basketball, you know that most of them have a tendency to dribble with only one hand—the one attached to their dominant arm.

When you notice a child doing this, you might call him aside and say, "Billy, you're dribbling with just the one hand every time, and the defender can easily defend you when you do that. Your options are cut off. You need to dribble with your other hand, too, so that he never knows which way you're going to go."

At this point Billy might say, "I can't." And you smile and say, "What do you mean you can't?"

And Billy then shows you that when he dribbles with his subdominant (weaker) hand and arm, the ball is all over the place. So, to his mind, he can't.

"Billy," you say. "It's not that you *can't*, it's just that you *haven't*."

Then you explain to Billy that his other hand can dribble just as well if he is willing to practice. It's just a matter of logging enough bounces. It's the simple formation of a habit. After enough practice dribbling with his other hand, Billy will learn you were right.

The same principle is true for reprogramming our own dominant habits of thinking. If our dominant thought habit is pessimistic, all we have to do is dribble with the other hand: Think optimistic thoughts more and more often until it feels natural.

If someone had asked me (before I started my journey to self-motivation that began with Napoleon Hill) why I didn't try to be more goal oriented and optimistic, I would have said, "I can't. It's just not me. I wouldn't know how." But it would have been more accurate for me to just say, "I haven't."

Thinking is just like bouncing the basketball. On the one hand, I can think pessimistically and build that side of me up (it's just a matter of repeatedly bouncing those thoughts). On the other hand, I can think optimistically—one thought at a time—and build *that* habit up. Self-motivation is all a matter of how much in control you want to be.

I read somewhere that we humans have up to 45,000 thoughts a day. I can't vouch for the accuracy of that figure, especially because I know some people who seem to have no more than nine or 10. However, if it is true that we have 45,000 thoughts, then you can see how patient we have to be about turning a pessimistic thought habit around.

The overall pattern won't change after just a few positive bounces of the brain. If you're a pessimist, your bio-computer has really been programmed heavily in that direction. But it doesn't take long before a new pattern can emerge. As a former pessimist myself, I can tell you it really happens, however slowly but surely. You do change. One thought at a time.

If you can bounce it one way, you can bounce it the other.

15. Light your lazy dynamite

Henry Ford used to point out to his colleagues that there wasn't any job that couldn't be handled if they were willing to break it down into little pieces.

And when you've broken a job down, remember to allow yourself some slow motion in beginning the first piece. Just take it slow and easy. Because it isn't important how fast you are doing it. What's important is *that* you are doing it.

Most of our hardest jobs never seem to get done. The mere thought of doing the whole job, at a high energy level, is frequently too off-putting to allow motivation to occur.

But a good way to ease yourself into that motivation is to act as if you were the laziest person on the planet. (It wasn't much of an act for me!) By accepting that you're going to do your task in a slow and lazy way, there is no anxiety or dread about getting it started. In fact, you can even have fun by entering into it as if you were in a slow-motion comedy, flowing into the work like a person made of water.

But the paradox is that the slower you start something, the faster you will be finished.

When you first think about doing something hard or overwhelming, you are most aware of how you don't want to do it at all. In other words, the mental picture you have of the activity, of doing it fast and furiously, is not a happy picture. So you think of ways to avoid doing the job altogether.

The thought of starting slowly is an easy thought. And doing it slowly allows you to actually start doing it. Therefore it gets finished.

Another thing that happens when you flow into a project slowly is that speed will often overtake you without your forcing it. Just as the natural rhythm inside you will get you in sync with what you are doing. You'll be surprised how soon your conscious mind stops forcing the action and your subconscious mind supplies you with easy energy.

So take your time. Start out lazy. Soon your tasks will be keeping the slow but persistent rhythm of that hypnotic song on Paul McCartney's *Red Rose Speedway* album, "Oh Lazy Dynamite."

The dynamite is living inside you. You don't have to be frenzied about setting it off. It lights just as well to a match struck slowly.

16. Choose the happy few

Politely walk away from friends who don't support the changes in your life.

There will be friends who don't. They will be jealous and afraid every time you make a change. They will see your new motivation as a condemnation of their own lack of it. In subtle ways, they will bring you back down to who you used to be. Beware of friends and family who do this. They know not what they do.

The people you spend time with will change your life in one way or another. If you associate with cynics, they'll pull you down with them. If you associate with people who support you in being happy and successful, you will have a head start on being happy and successful.

Throughout the day we have many choices regarding who we are going to be with and talk to. Don't just gravitate to the coffee machine and participate in the negative gossip because it's the only game in town. It will drain your energy and stifle your own optimism. We all know who lifts us up, and we all know who brings us down. It's okay to start being more careful about to whom we give our time.

In his inspiring book *Spontaneous Healing*, Andrew Weil recommends: "Make a list of friends and acquaintances in whose company you feel more alive, happier, more optimistic. Pick one whom you will spend some time with this week."

When you're in a conversation with a cynic, possibilities seem to have a way of disappearing. A mildly depressing sense of fatalism seems to take over the conversation. No new ideas and no innovative humor.

"Cynics," observed President Calvin Coolidge, "do not create."

On the other hand, enthusiasm for life is contagious. And being in a conversation with an optimist always opens us up to see more and more of life's possibilities.

Kierkegaard once said, "If I were to wish for anything, I should not wish for wealth and power, but for the passionate sense of the potential, for the eye which, ever young and ardent, sees the possible. Pleasure disappoints, possibility never."

17. Learn to play a role

Your future is not determined by your personality. In fact, your personality is not even determined by your personality. There is no genetic code in you that determines who you will be. *You are the thinker* who determines who you will be. How you *act* is who you become.

Another way of seeing that might be contained in these related thoughts from *Star Trek*'s Leonard Nimoy: "Spock had a big, big effect on me. I am so much more Spock-like today than when I first played the part in 1965 that you wouldn't recognize me. I'm not talking about appearance, but *thought* processes. Doing that character, I learned so much about rational logical thought that it reshaped my life."

You'll gather energy and inspiration by being the character *you* want to play.

I took an acting class a few years ago because I thought it would help me deal with my overwhelming stage fright. But I learned something much more valuable than how to relax in front of a crowd. I learned that my emotions were tools for me to use, not demonic forces. I learned that my emotions were mine to work with and change at will.

Although I had *read* countless times that our own deliberate thoughts control our emotions, and that the feelings we have are all caused by what we think, I never trusted that concept as real, because it didn't always feel real.

To me, it felt more like emotion was an all-powerful thing that could overcome my thinking and ruin a good day (or a good relationship).

It took a great acting teacher, Judy Rollings, and my own long struggles with performing difficult scenes to show me that my emotions really could be under the complete control of my mind. I found out that I could motivate myself by thinking and acting like a motivated person, just as I could depress myself by thinking and acting like a depressed person. With practice, the fine line between acting and being disappeared.

We love great actors because it seems like they *are* the characters they play. Poor actors are those who can't "be" their part and therefore don't convince us of their character's reality. We hoot at those people. We call it bad acting.

Yet we don't realize that we ourselves miss the same opportunities in life when we can't "be" the person *we* want to be. It doesn't take authentic circumstances to be who you want to be. It just takes rehearsal.

18. Don't just do something...sit there

For a long time, all by yourself, sit quietly, absolutely alone. Completely relax. Don't allow the television or music to be on. Just be with yourself. Watch for what happens. Feel your sense of belonging to the silence. Observe insights starting to appear. Observe your relationship with yourself starting to get better and softer and more comfortable.

Sitting quietly allows your true dream life to give you hints and flashes of motivation. In this information-rich, interactive, civilized life today, you are either living your dream or living someone else's. And unless you give your own dream the time and space it needs to formulate itself, you'll spend the better part of your life simply helping others make *their* dreams come true.

"All of man's troubles," said Blaise Pascal, "stem from his inability to sit alone, quietly, in a room for any length of time."

Notice that he did not say *some* of man's troubles, but *all*.

Sometimes, in my seminars on motivation, a person will ask me, "Why is it that I get my best ideas when I'm in the shower?"

I usually ask the person, "When else during your day are you alone with yourself, without any distractions?"

If the person is honest, the answer is *never*.

Great ideas come to us in the shower when it's the only time in the day when we're completely alone. No television, no movies, no traffic, no radio, no family, no talkative pets—nothing to distract our mind from conversing with itself.

"Thinking," said Plato, "is the soul talking to itself."

People worry they will die of boredom or fear if they are alone for any length of time. Other people have become so distraction-addicted that they would consider sitting alone by themselves like being in a sensory-deprivation tank.

The truth is that the only real motivation we ever experience is *self*-motivation that comes from within. And being alone with ourselves will always give us motivating ideas if we stay with the process long enough.

The best way to truly understand the world is to remove yourself from it. Psychic entropy—the seesaw mood swing between boredom and anxiety—occurs when you allow yourself to become confused by massive input. By being perpetually busy, glued to your cell phone, out in the world all day with no time to reflect, you will guarantee yourself an eventual overwhelming sense of confusion.

The cure is simple and painless. The process is uncomplicated.

"You do not need to leave your room," said Franz Kafka. "Remain sitting at your table and listen. Do not even listen. Simply wait. Do not even wait. Be quite still and solitary. The world will freely offer itself to you to be unmasked. It has no choice, it will roll in ecstasy at your feet."

In other words, don't just do something...sit there.

19. Use your brain chemicals

There are drugs that you can use to motivate yourself with, and I'm not talking about amphetamine or crack (a deadly form of child's play).

Instead, you can get into those energizing chemicals in your system that get activated when you laugh...or sing...or dance...or run...or hug someone. When you're having fun, your body chemistry changes and you get new biochemical surges of motivation and energy.

And there isn't anything you do that can't be transformed into something interesting and uplifting. Victor Frankl has written startling accounts of his life in the Nazi concentration camps, and how some prisoners created new universes unto themselves inside their own minds. It might sound absurd, but truly imaginative people can access their inner chemical creativity in the loneliness of a prison cell.

Don't keep trying to go outside yourself searching for something that's fun. It's not out there anywhere. It's inside. The opportunity for fun is in your own energy system—your synergy of heart and mind. That's where you'll find it.

Pro football Hall of Famer Fran Tarkenton recommends looking at any task you do as fun.

"If it's not fun," he says, "you're not doing it right."

People who get high on marijuana often find they can laugh at anything. The problem with them is that they think this kind of "fun" is inherent in the marijuana. It's not. The capacity for fun was already there inside of them. The marijuana just artificially opened them up to it. But the physical and psychological price paid for such a drugged opening is not worth the high. (I wish I didn't know this first hand, but I do.) The price drug users pay is this: Their self-esteem suffers because they didn't *create* the fun they had—they thought the drugs did it for them. So they keep shrinking, the more they use, into greater paranoia and self-disgust. Soon they're using the drug just to feel normal.

William Burroughs, a former drug addict and author of *Naked Lunch,* discovered something that was very interesting and bitterly amusing to him after finally recovering from his addictions.

"There isn't any feeling you can get on drugs," he said "that you can't get without drugs."

Make a commitment to yourself to find the *natural* highs you need to stay motivated. Start by finding out what it does to your mood and energy to laugh, to sing, to dance, to walk, to run, to hug someone, or to get something done.

Then support your experiments by telling yourself that you're not interested in doing *anything* that isn't fun. If you can't immediately see the fun in something, find a way to create it. Once you have made a task fun, you have solved the problem of self-motivation.

20. Leave high school forever

Most of us feel like we've been left stranded in high school forever. Like something happened there that we've never shaken off.

Before high school, in our earlier and more carefree childhoods, we were creative dreamers filled with a boundless sense of energy and wonder.

But in high school something got turned around. For the first time in our lives, we began fearing what other people were thinking of us. All of a sudden our mission in life became *not to be embarrassed.* We were afraid to look bad, and so we made it a point not to take risks.

I'll never forget something that happened to my friend, Richard Schwarze, in high school. (He is now a respected photographer, and I won't need to ask his permission to tell this story about him.) Richard and I were walking home from school one day and all of a sudden he stopped in his tracks, his face frozen with horror. I looked at him and asked what was wrong. I thought he was about to suffer some kind of seizure. He then pointed down at his pants and wordlessly showed me where his belt had missed a loop!

"I spent the whole *day* like this!" he finally said. It was impossible for him to measure what everybody thought of him as they passed him in the halls, perhaps seeing the belt had missed a loop. The damage to his reputation was probably beyond repair.

That was high school.

Today when I give my seminars on motivation, I love the periods when I take questions from the audience. But many times I can see the painfully adolescent looks of self-consciousness on people's faces when they ponder the risk of asking a question in front of the group.

This habit of worrying more about what others think of our thoughts than we do about our own thinking usually begins in high school, but it can last a lifetime.

It is time to be aware of what we're doing and, once again, leave high school. It's time to reach back to those pre-high-school days of innocent creativity and social fearlessness, and draw on that former self.

By the way, I finally came up with a way to deal with the moments of silence that fill a seminar room when I ask for questions. I go to the board and make five circles. Then I tell the audience that I used to say in my classes, "If there are no questions at this point, we'll take a break." People always want to take a break, so there wasn't much incentive for asking questions. But questions are the most fun part of a seminar for me, so I came up with this game: *After five questions—we take a break.* Now I find people in the audience urging people around them to join in asking questions so we can take our break sooner. Although it's an amusing artificial way to jump-start the dialogue I'm looking for, what it really does is take the pressure off. It takes the participants out of high school.

Most people don't realize how easily they can create the social fearlessness they want to have. Instead, they live like they are still teenagers, reacting to the imagined judgments of other people. They end up designing their lives based on what other people might be thinking about them. A life designed by a teenager! Would you want one?

But you can leave that mind-set behind. You can motivate yourself by yourself, without depending on the opinions of others. All it takes is a simple question. As Emerson asked, "Why should the way I feel depend on the thoughts in someone else's head?"

21. Learn to lose your cool

You can create a self that doesn't care that much about what people think. You can motivate yourself by leaving the painful self-consciousness of high school behind.

Because our tendency is to go so far in the timid, non-assertive direction, it might be a profitable over-correction to adopt these internal commands: Look bad. Take a risk. Lose face. Be yourself. Share yourself with someone. Open up. Be vulnerable. Be human. Leave your comfort zone. Get honest. Experience the fear. Do it anyway.

"Show me a guy who's afraid to look bad," said actor Rene Auberjonois, "and I'll show you a guy you can beat every time."

The first time that I ever spoke to author and psychotherapist Devers Branden it was over the telephone, and she agreed to work with me on building my own self-confidence and personal growth. It wasn't long into the phone conversation before she asked me about my voice.

"I am very interested in your voice," she said, with a tone of curiosity.

Hoping she might be ready to give me a compliment I asked her to explain.

"Well," she said. "It's so lifeless. A real monotone. I wonder why that is."

Embarrassed, I had no explanation. This conversation took place long before I had become a professional speaker, and it was also long before I ever took any acting lessons. It was long before I learned to sing in my car, too. Yet I was completely unaware and very surprised that it seemed to her that I was coming across with a voice like someone out of *Night of the Living Dead.*

The truth was that during that period in my life, I was living scared. Things weren't going well for me financially, I had serious health problems in my family, and I had that mildly suicidal feeling that accompanies an increasing sense of powerlessness over one's problems. (I now think one way a lot of men hide their fears is by assuming a macho kind of dull indifference. I know now that's what I had done. That a psychotherapist could hear it immediately in my voice was unnerving, though.)

Trying to understand why I covered fear with indifference, I remembered that back in my high school the "cool" guys were always the least enthusiastic guys. They spoke in monotones, emulating their heroes James Dean and Marlon Brando. Brando was the coolest of all. He was so indifferent and unenthusiastic you couldn't even understand him when he spoke.

One of the first homework assignments Devers Branden gave me was to rent the video *Gone with the Wind* and study how fearlessly Clark Gable revealed his female side. This sounded weird to me. Gable a *female*? I knew Gable was always considered a true "man's man" in all those old movies, so I couldn't understand what Devers was talking about, or how it would help me.

But when I watched the movie, it became strangely clear. Clark Gable allowed himself such a huge emotional range of expression, that I could actually identify scenes where he was revealing a distinctly female side to his character's personality. Did it make him less manly? No. Curiously, it made him more real, and more compelling.

From that time on, I lost my desire to hide myself behind an indifferent monotonous person. I committed myself to get on the road to creating a self that included a wider range of expression, without a nervous preoccupation with coming off like a man's man.

I also started noticing how much we seem to love vulnerability in others but don't trust it in ourselves.

But we can learn to trust it!

Just a little at first. Then we can build that vulnerability until we're not afraid to open up into an ever-widening spectrum of self-revelation. By losing face, we connect to the real excitement of life. And what if I don't always come off as an indifferent man's man? Frankly, my dear, I don't give a damn.

22. Kill your television

My brother used to own a T-shirt store and one of the most popular shirts for sale said, "Kill Your Television." I bought that T-shirt with the picture of a TV being blown up. It still makes people nervous to look at it when I wear it today.

You can actually change your life by turning off your television. Maybe just one evening a week, to start with. What would happen if you stopped trying to find life in other people's shows and let your own life become the show you got hooked on?

Cutting down on television is sometimes terrifying to the electronically addicted, but don't be afraid. You can detox slowly. If you're watching too much television and you know it, you might find it useful to ask this one question: *"Which side of the glass do I want to live on?"*

When you are watching television you are watching other people do what they love doing for a living. Those people are on the smart side of the glass, because they are having fun, and you are passively watching them have fun. They are getting money, and you are not.

There's nothing *wrong* with occasionally watching other people do what they love doing. But the average household now does this for *seven hours* a day! Are they living on the side of the glass that will advance their lives? (Big advertisers hope not.)

Here's a good test for you to determine if television motivates you more than books do: Try to remember what you watched on television a month ago. Think hard. What effect are those shows having on the inspired side of your brain? Now think about the book that you read a month ago. Or even the e-zine you read last week. Which made a more valuable and lasting impression? Which form of entertainment better leads you in the direction of self-motivation?

Today the growing fascination with going online is an improvement over television, especially if you interact. Communicating inside thoughtful chat rooms and sending and receiving e-mail both grow the brain. Television does the opposite.

Groucho Marx once said he found television very educational. "Every time someone turns it on," he said, "I go in the other room to read a book."

23. Break out of your soul cage

Our society encourages us to seek comfort. Most products and services advertised day and night are designed to make us more comfortable and less challenged.

And yet, only *challenge* causes growth. Only *challenge* will test our skills and make us better. Only challenge and the self-motivation to engage the challenge will transform us. Every challenge we face is an opportunity to create a more skillful self.

So it is up to you to constantly look for challenges to motivate yourself with. And it's up to you to notice when you're buried alive in a comfort zone. It's up to you to notice when you are spending your life, in the image of the poet William Olsen, like a flower "living under the wind."

Use your comfort zones to rest in, not to live in. Use them consciously to relax and restore your energy as you mentally prepare for your next challenge. But if you use comfort zones to live in forever, they become what rock singer Sting calls your "soul cages." Break free. Fly away. Experience what the philosopher Fichte meant when he said, "Being free is nothing. Becoming free is heavenly."

24. Run your own plays

Design your own life's game plan. Let the game respond to you rather than the other way around. Be like Bill Walsh, the former head coach of the San Francisco 49ers. Everybody thought he was a kind of eccentric because of how extensively he planned his plays in advance of each game. Most coaches would wait to see how the game unfolded, then respond with plays that reacted to the other team. Not Bill Walsh. Walsh would pace the sidelines with a big sheet of plays that his team was going to run, no matter what. He wanted the other team to respond to *him*.

Walsh won a lot of Super Bowls with his unorthodox proactive approach. But all he did was to act on the crucial difference between creating and reacting.

You can create your own plans in advance so that your life will respond to *you*. If you can hold the thought that at all times your life is either a creation or a reaction, you can continually remind yourself to be creating and planning. "Creation" and "reaction" have the same letters in them, exactly; they are anagrams. (Perhaps that's why people slip so easily out of one and into the other.)

Many of us can spend whole days reacting without being aware of it. We wake up reacting to news on the clock radio. Then we react to feelings in our body. Then we start reacting to our spouses or our children. Soon we get in the car and react to traffic, honking the horn and using sign language. Then, at work, we see an e-mail on our computer screen and react to that. We react to stupid customers and insensitive bosses who are intruding on our day. During a break, we react to a waitress at lunch.

This habit of reacting can go on all day, every day. We become goalies in the hockey game of life, with pucks flying at us incessantly.

It's time to play another position. It's time to fly across the ice with the puck on our own stick ready to shoot at another goal.

Robert Fritz, who has written some of the most profound and useful books on the differences between creating and reacting, says, "When your life itself becomes the subject matter of the creative process, a very different experience of life opens to you—one in which you are involved with life at its very essence."

Plan your day the way Bill Walsh planned his football games. See the tasks ahead as plays you're going to run. You'll feel involved in your life at its very essence, because you'll be encouraging the world to respond to *you*. If you don't choose to do that, the life you get won't be an accident. As an old Jewish folk saying puts it, "A person who does not make a choice makes a choice."

25. Find your inner Einstein

The next time you see a picture of Albert Einstein, realize that that's actually you. See Albert Einstein and say, "there I am."

Every human has the capacity for some form of genius. You don't have to be good with math or physics to experience genius level in your thinking. To experience Einstein's creative level of thinking, all you have to do is habitually use your imagination.

This is a difficult recommendation for adults to follow, though, because adults have become accustomed to using their imaginations for only one thing: worrying. Adults visualize worst-case scenarios all day long. All their energy for visualization is channeled into colorful pictures of what they dread.

What they don't comprehend is that worry is a *misuse* of the imagination. The human imagination was designed for better things. People who use their imaginations to *create* with often achieve things that worriers never dream of achieving, even if the worriers possess much higher IQs. People who habitually access their imaginations are often hailed by their colleagues as "geniuses"—as if "genius" was a genetic characteristic. They would be better understood as people who are practiced at *accessing* their genius.

Recognition of the power of this genius in all of us prompted Napoleon to say, "Imagination rules the world."

As a child, you instinctively used your imagination as it was intended. You daydreamed and made stuff up. You were a daydream believer by day and in your right brain at night you sailed down a river of dreams.

If you go back into that state of self-confidence and dream again, you'll be pleasantly surprised at how many innovative and immediate solutions you come up with to your problems.

Einstein used to say, "Imagination is more important than knowledge." When I first heard he'd said that, I didn't know what he meant. I always thought additional *knowledge* was the answer to every difficult problem. I thought if I could just learn a few more important things, then I'd be okay. What I didn't realize was that the very thing I needed to learn was not knowledge, but skill. What I needed to learn was the skill of proactively using my imagination.

And once I'd learned that skill, the first task was to begin imagining the vision of who I wanted to be. Songwriter Fred Knipe once wrote a song about this. It was for the soundtrack of a video produced for teenagers about how to visualize themselves succeeding at what they wanted to do:

"That's you / in your wildest dreams / doing the wildest things / no one else can do. If you / just love and keep those dreams / the wildest dreams / you'll make yourself come true."

To make ourselves come true we need to develop the strength to dream. Dreaming, in its proactive sense, is strong work. It's the design stage of creating the future. It takes confidence and it takes courage. But the greatest thing about active dreaming is not in the eventual reaching of the goal—the greatest thing is what it does to the dreamer.

Forget the literal attainment of your dream for now. Focus on just going for it. By simply going for the dream, you make *yourself* come true.

26. Run toward your fear

The world's best-kept secret is that on the other side of your fear there is something safe and beneficial waiting for you. If you pass through even a thin curtain of fear you will increase the confidence you have in your ability to create your life.

General George Patton said, "Fear kills more people than death." Death kills us but once, and we usually don't even know it. But fear kills us over and over again, subtly at times and brutally at others. But if we keep trying to avoid our fears, they will chase us down like persistent dogs. The worst thing we can do is close our eyes and pretend they don't exist.

"Fear and pain," says psychologist Nathaniel Branden, "should be treated as signals not to close our eyes but to open them wider." By closing our eyes we end up in the darkest of comfort zones—buried alive.

Janis Joplin's biography, which chronicled her death from alcohol and drug abuse, was aptly titled *Buried Alive.* To Janis, as to so many similarly troubled people, alcohol provided an artificial and tragically temporary antidote to fear. It is no accident that in the old frontier days the nickname for whiskey was "false courage."

There was a time in my life, not too many years ago, when my greatest fear of all was public speaking. It didn't even help that fear of speaking in front of people was people's number one fear, even greater than the fear of death. This fact once caused comedian Jerry Seinfeld to point out that most people would rather be in the coffin than delivering the eulogy.

For me, it ran even deeper than that. As a child I could not give oral book reports. I'd plead with my teachers to let me off the hook. I would offer to do two, even three *written* book reports if I didn't have to do the oral one.

Yet as my life went on, I wanted to be a public speaker more than anything. My dream was to teach people everywhere to learn the ideas that lead to self-motivation, the ideas that I had learned. But how could I ever do this if stage fright left me frozen with fear?

Then one day as I was driving in Phoenix flipping through the radio stations looking for good music, I accidentally happened upon a religious station where a histrionic preacher was yelling, "Run toward your fear! Run right at it!" I hastened to change the station, but it was too late. Deep down I knew that I had just heard something I needed to hear. No matter what station I turned to, all I could hear was that madman's words: "Run toward your fear!"

The next day I still couldn't get it out of my mind, so I called a friend of mine who was an actress. I asked her to help me get into an acting class she had once told me about. I told her I thought I was ready to overcome my fear of performing in front of people.

Although I lived in a high state of anxiety the first weeks of that class, there was no other way around my fear. There was no real way to run from it any longer, because the more I ran, the more pervasive it got. I knew I had to turn around and run *toward* the fear or I would never pass through it.

Emerson once said, "The greater part of courage is having done it before," and that soon became true of my speaking in public. Fear of doing it can only be cured by doing it. And soon my confidence was built by doing it again and again.

The rush we get after running through the waterfall of fear is the most energizing feeling in the world. If you are ever in an undermotivated mood, find something you fear and do it—and watch what happens.

27. Create the way you relate

We can't create our truest selves without creating relationships in the process. Relationships are everywhere. Relationships are everything.

"There is no end to relationship," said the Indian spiritual leader Krishnamurti. "There may be the end of a particular relationship, but relationship can never end. To be is to be related."

I have trained many corporations with a four-part seminar series. The first three parts are on self-motivation, and the final part is on relationship building. Sometimes CEOs ask me up front, ahead of the training, if I don't have that ratio out of balance.

"Shouldn't you have more of it be on relationship building?" they ask. "After all, team-building and customer relations are surely more important than self-motivation."

I stand by my ratio. We can't relate to others if our relationship with ourselves is poor. A commitment to personal motivation comes first. Because who wants to have a relationship with someone who is not motivated in any way?

When we do get to the fourth part, relationship building, the focus is on creativity. Creativity is the most neglected and yet most useful aspect of relationship building.

In relationships most of us think with our emotions rather than our minds. But to think with our feelings instead of our minds puts us in the unresourceful state that Colin Wilson describes as being upside-down.

When we view relationships as opportunities for creativity, they always get better. When our relationships get better, we are even more motivated.

My youngest daughter, Margie, was in fourth grade when a very shy girl in her class accidentally put a large black mark on her own nose with an indelible marker. Many of the kids in the class pointed at her and started to laugh. The little girl was finally reduced to tears of embarrassment.

At some point Margie walked over to the girl to give her some comfort. (Margie's astonished teacher related this story to me.) Impulsively, Margie picked up the marker and marked her own nose, and then handed the marker to another classmate and said, "I like my nose this way. What about you?"

In a few moments the entire class had black marks on their noses, and the shy girl who was once crying was laughing. At recess, Margie's class all went out on the playground with marked noses, and they were the envy of the school—obviously into something unusual and "cool."

This story is interesting to me because of how Margie used her creativity and her mind instead of her emotions to solve a problem. She elevated herself up into her mind, where something clever could be done. If she had used her feelings to think with, she might have expressed anger at the class for laughing at the girl, or sadness and depression.

Any time you take a relationship problem up into the mind, you have unlimited opportunities to get creative. Conversely, when you send a relationship problem down the elevator into the lower half of the heart, you risk staying stuck in the problem forever.

This doesn't mean that you shouldn't feel anything. Feel everything! Notice your feelings. Just don't think with them. When there's a relationship problem to be solved, travel up your ladder to the most creative you. You'll soon realize that we *create* the relationships we have in our lives; they don't just happen.

"We are each of us angels with only one wing," said the Italian artist Luciano de Crescenzo, "and we can only fly embracing each other."

28. Try interactive listening

The principle of using interactivity as a creativity-builder is not restricted to computer games or chat rooms. Once we become fully conscious of this principle, we can find ways to become more interactive everywhere. We can even make conversations with our family and friends more interactive than they once were.

We all have certain business associates or family members that we think of as we do television sets. As they speak to us, we have a feeling that we already know what they're going to say. This lowers our own consciousness level, and a form of mental laziness sets in.

Whereas in the past we might have just passively suffered through other people's monologues, we can now begin introducing more interactivity. In the past we might have punctuated our sleepy listening with meaningless words and phrases, such as "exactly" and "there you go," but we weren't truly listening. But that passive approach shortchanges ourselves and the people we are listening to.

"When we are listened to," wrote Brenda Ueland, "it creates us, makes us unfold and expand. Ideas actually begin to grow within us and come to life."

The more thoughtful our questions get to be, the more interactive the conversations. Look for opportunities for interactivity to motivate yourself to higher levels of experience.

29. Embrace your willpower

I can't tell you how many people have told me that they have no willpower. Do you think the same thing? If you think you have no willpower, you are undermining your own success. Everyone has willpower. To be reading this sentence, you must have willpower.

The first step in developing your willpower, therefore, is to accept its existence. You have willpower just as surely as you have life.

If someone were to put a large barbell weight on the floor in front of you and ask you to lift it and you knew you could not, you would not say "I have no strength." You'd say, "I'm not strong *enough*."

Not strong "enough" is more truthful language, because it implies that you *could* be strong enough if you worked at it. It also implies that *you do have strength.*

It is the same with willpower. Of course you have willpower. When you accept that little piece of chocolate cake, it is not because you have no willpower. It is only because you choose not to exercise it in that instance.

The first step toward building willpower is to celebrate the fact that you've got it. You've got willpower, just like that muscle in your arm. It might not be a very strong muscle, but you do have that muscle.

The second step is to know that your willpower, like a muscle in your arm, is yours to develop. You are in charge of making it strong or letting it atrophy. It is not grown by random external circumstances. Willpower is a deliberate volitional process.

When I left college to join the army, one of the reasons I decided to sign up was because I thought it might help teach me to develop my self-discipline. But somehow I had not been aware of the "self" in self-discipline. I wanted discipline to be *given* to me by someone else. I found out in boot camp that others do not give willpower and self-discipline. The drill sergeant might have been persuasive and inspiring (or at times terrifying), but he couldn't *make* me do anything until I decided to do it. Nothing happened until *I* generated the will to make it happen.

Make a promise to yourself to be clear and truthful about your own willpower. It is always there.

30. Perform your little rituals

See yourself as a shaman or medicine man who needs to dance and sing to get the healing started.

Make up a ritual that is yours and yours alone—a ritual that will be your own shortcut to self-motivation.

As you read through these various ways to motivate yourself, you might have noticed that action is often the key. *Doing something* is what leads to doing something. It's a law of the universe: An object in motion stays in motion.

The great basketball player Jack Twyman used to begin each practice session by getting to the court early and taking 200 shots at the basket. It always had to be 200 shots, which he counted out, and it didn't matter if he already felt tuned up after 20 or 30 shots. He had to shoot 200. It was his ritual, and it always got him into a state of self-motivation for the rest of the practice session or game.

My friend Fred Knipe, now an Emmy award-winning television writer and comedian, does something he calls "driving for ideas." When he has a major creative project to accomplish, he gets in his car and drives around the desert near Tucson until ideas begin to come to him. His theory is that the act of driving gives the anxious, logical left side of his brain something to do so the right side of his brain can be freed up to suggest ideas. It's like giving your child some toys to play with so you can read the evening e-mail on your computer.

In his book about songwriting, *Write from the Heart*, John Stewart writes about composer and arranger Glenn Gould, who had a ritual for finding a new melody or musical idea when he seemed to be stuck and nothing was coming. He'd turn on two or three radios at the same time, all to different stations. He'd sit and compose his own music while listening to music on the three radios. This would short-circuit his conscious mind and free up the creative subconscious. It would overload the left side of his brain so the right could open up and create without judgment.

My own ritual for jump-starting self-motivation is walking. Many times in my life I have had a problem that seemed too overwhelming to do anything about, and my ritual is to take the problem out for a long, long walk. Sometimes I won't come back for hours. But time and again during the course of my walks something comes out of nowhere—some idea for an action that will quickly solve the problem.

One of the reasons I think this ritual works for me is that a ritual *is* action. Starting a ritual is taking an action that leads toward finding the solution. The dancing medicine man is already doing something.

Make up little rituals for yourself that will act as self-starters. They will have you in action before you "feel like" getting into action. Rituals always override your built-in hesitation so that you can get yourself motivated in a predictable, controllable way.

If you are not a writer or painter or poet, you might be thinking right now that this does not apply to you. But that's what I would call the creative fallacy. In fact, your entire life is yours to create. There are no "creative" professions that stand apart from others, like an exclusive club.

Martin Luther King Jr. used to say, "Be an artist at whatever you do. Even if you are a street sweeper, be the Michelangelo of street sweepers!"

31. Find a place to come from

Most people think they'll feel good once they reach some goal. They think happiness is *out there* somewhere, perhaps not even too far away, but out there all the same.

The problem with putting off feeling good about yourself until you hit a certain goal is that it may never happen. And you know all the time you're striving for it that it may never happen. So, by linking your happiness to something you don't have yet, you're denying your power to create happiness for yourself.

A lot of people use personal *unhappiness* as a tool, as proof of their own sincerity and compassion. Yet, as Barry Kaufman points out eloquently in *To Love Is to Be Happy With*, being unhappy is not necessary. You can be happy and also be sincere. You can be happy and also be compassionate. In fact, loving someone while you are *un*happy does not show up like love at all.

"Love," says the great American spiritual teacher, Emmet Fox, "acts the part."

Songwriter Fred Knipe talked to me recently about how we human beings have learned to use and abuse unhappiness—he said he had made a list for me of the secret reasons why people think they *should* feel bad.

"If I feel bad, then that proves I am a good person," he said. "Or, if I feel bad, I am responsible. If I feel bad, I'm not hurting anybody. If I feel bad, it means that I care. Maybe if I feel bad, it proves I'm being realistic and aware. If I feel bad, it means I'm working on something."

That list gives us powerful motivation to be *unhappy*. But as Werner Erhard (personal transformation pioneer) has always taught in his well-known *est* seminars, happiness is a place to come from, not to try to go to.

I once saw Larry King interviewing Werner Erhard by satellite from Russia, where Erhard was living and working. Erhard had mentioned that he might be moving back to the United States soon, and Larry King asked him if coming home would make him happy.

Erhard paused uncomfortably, because in his view of life nothing *makes us* happy. He finally said, "Larry, I am already happy. That wouldn't make me happy, because I come from happiness to whatever I do."

Your happiness is your birthright. It shouldn't depend on your achieving something. Start by claiming it and using it to make your self-motivation fun *all the way* and not just fun at the end.

32. Be your own disciple

So, why *do* I claim we have no willpower? Is it a misguided desire to protect myself? Is there a secret payoff in saying I have no willpower? Maybe if I absolutely deny the existence of willpower, I am no longer responsible for developing it. It's out of my life! What a relief!

But, here's the final tragedy: The development and use of willpower is the most direct access to happiness and motivation that I'll ever have. In short, by denying its existence, I'm shutting my spirit down.

Many people think of willpower and self-discipline as something akin to self-punishment. By giving it that negative connotation, they never get enthused about developing it. But author William Bennett gives us a different way to think of it. Self-discipline, he notes in *The Book of Virtues*, comes from the word "disciple." When you are self-disciplined, you have simply decided—in matters of the will—to become your own disciple.

Once you make that decision, your life's adventure gets more interesting. You start to see yourself as a stronger person. You gain self-respect.

American philosopher Ralph Waldo Emerson used to talk about the Sandwich Island warriors who believed that when they killed an enemy tribesman, the courage of that dead enemy passed into the warrior's living body. Emerson said that the same thing happens to us when we say no to a temptation. The power of that dead temptation passes into us. It strengthens our will.

When we resist a small temptation, we take on a small power. When we resist a huge temptation, we take on huge power.

William James recommended that we do at least two *things* every day that we don't want to do—for the very reason that we don't want to do them—just to keep willpower alive. By doing this, we maintain our awareness of our own will.

33. Turn into a word processor

If you associate the word "willpower" with negative things, such as harsh self-denial and punishment, you will weaken your resolve to build it. To increase your resolve, it's often useful to think of new word associations.

To weight lifters, *failure is success*. Unless they lift a weight to the point of "failure," their muscles aren't growing. So they have programmed themselves, through repetition, to use the word "failure" in a positive sense.

They also call what we would call "pain" something positive: "the burn." Getting to "the burn" is the goal! You'll hear bodybuilders call out to each other: "Roast 'em!" By consciously using motivated language, they acquire access to inner power through the use of the human will.

Zen philosopher and scholar Alan Watts also used to hate the word "discipline" because it had so many negative connotations. Yet he knew that the key to enjoying *any* activity was in the discipline. So he would substitute the word "skill" for "discipline" and when he did that he was able to develop his own self-discipline.

Language leads to power, so be conscious of the creative potential of the language you use, and guide it in the direction of more personal power.

34. Program your biocomputer

If you're a regular consumer of the major news programs, you belong to a very persuasive and hypnotic cult. You need to be de-"programmed."

Start by altering how you listen to electronic radio gossip, the news, and shock and schlock TV shows. Program out all the negative, cynical, and skeptical thoughts that you now allow to flow into your mind unchecked when you hear the news.

"Headless Woman Found in Topless Bar!"

That was an actual headline in a daily New York City newspaper. I used to work for a city newspaper, and I remember how hard the editors in the newsroom would search for the most shocking stories they could find.

The news is not the news. It is the *bad news*. It is deliberate shock. The more you accept it as the news, the more you believe that "that's the way it is," and the more fearful and cynical you will become.

If we realized exactly how much vulgar, pessimistic, and manipulative negativity was deliberately packed into every daily newspaper and most television shows and Hollywood movies, we would resist the temptation to flood our brains with their garbage. Most of us are more particular about what we put in our automobile's gas tank than we are about what we put in our own brain every night. We passively feed ourselves with stories about serial killers and violent crime without any conscious awareness of the choice we're making.

How do we change it? By worrying about it? No. Rather than fretting about crime and apathy and whatever you wish would change in the world, it's often very motivational to heed the words of Gandhi, who said, "You must *be* the change you wish to see."

San Francisco writer and musician Gary Lachman wrote a captivating essay called "World Rejection and Criminal Romantics" in which he observed, "It's the Ted Bundys that get television coverage, not the thousands of self-actualizers who work away at self-transformation quietly and anonymously. And it's their influence, not that of the Ted Bundys, that will shape the face of the coming century."

Often we don't have an opportunity to skip the media reports of crime and scandal, so it's important that we listen in a way that always programs out the effect. We are pretty good at doing this when we pass the tabloids in the grocery store checkout line. We smile at them even before reading that aliens are living in the White House. We need to take that same attitude toward what passes as "serious" media.

Once you've gotten good at factoring out the negative aspects of the media today, take it a step further: Make your own news. Be your own breaking story. Don't look to the media to tell you what's happening in your life. *Be* what's happening.

35. Open your present

Practice being awake in the present moment. Make the most of your awareness of this hour. Don't live in the past (unless you want guilt) or worry about the future (unless you want fear), but stay focused on today (in case you want happiness).

"Until you can put your attention where you want it," said Emmet Fox, "you have not become master of yourself. You will never be happy until you can determine what you are going to think about for the next hour."

There is a time for dreaming, planning, and creative goal setting. But once you are complete with that, learn to live in the here and now. See your whole life as being contained in this very hour. Let the microcosm become the macrocosm. Live the words of the poet William Blake and his description of enlightenment:

"To see a world in a grain of sand

and heaven in a wild flower

hold infinity in the palm of your hand

and eternity in an hour."

Sir Walter Scott said he would trade whole years filled with mindless conformity for "*one hour* of life crowded to the full with glorious action, and filled with noble risks."

It's amazing what can be done by people who learn to relax, pay attention, and focus, appreciating the present hour and all the opportunity it contains.

It is said that in America we try to cultivate an appreciation of art, while the Japanese cultivate the art of appreciation. You, too, can cultivate the art of appreciation. Appreciate this hour. This hour, right now, is pure opportunity.

The great French philosopher Voltaire was on his deathbed when someone asked him, "If you had 24 more hours to live, how would you live them?" Voltaire said, "One at a time."

36. Be a good detective

In your professional life, whatever it is, always be curious. When you meet with someone, think of yourself as a bumbling but friendly private detective. Ask questions. Then ask follow-up questions. And then let the answers make you even more curious. Let the answers suggest even more questions. This will motivate you to higher levels of consciousness and interest.

When you prepare a meeting with someone, prepare your questions. Cultivate your curiosity. Don't ever be at a loss for questions to ask.

Most of us do the opposite. We prepare our *answers*. We rehearse what we are going to *say*. We polish our presentation, and strengthen it, not realizing that our host would much rather talk than listen to us.

If you are in business, you know that when prospective customers contract for long-term services, they want a company that's truly interested in them, that understands them, that will be a good consultant to them. To show a prospect that you are genuinely interested, you must be the person who asks the most thoughtful questions. To convince a company that you understand it, you will ask the best follow-up questions—based on its answers. To convince a company that you will be a good consultant to them over the course of the contract, you will have *out-learned* your competitors by the inventiveness and quantity of your questions. Your curiosity will get you the business. But you can't just rely on impulsive, on-the-spot questioning. Being prepared is the secret. Preparing your questions is even more important than preparing the presentation of your services.

Indiana's former basketball coach Bobby Knight always said, "The will to win is not as important as the will to prepare to win." This is not only useful in business. If you are about to have an important conversation with your spouse or teenager, it is very useful to prepare your curiosity rather than your presentation.

When you prepare your curiosity, you always seem to have one more question to ask before you leave, just like Lt. Columbo from the old TV show now showing in reruns on cable. As the character played by Peter Falk, Columbo disarmed his subjects by asking so many seemingly impromptu questions. Like a disorganized but innocently charming child, he would ask about the tiniest things. As he prepared to leave, he always paused at the door, as if absent-mindedly remembering something he forgot to ask. "Excuse me sir," he would say, apologetically. "Would it inconvenience you if I asked you one more question?"

Great relationship-builders ultimately learn that the sale most often goes to the most interested party and the quantity and quality of your questions will measure your level of interest. You might be thinking that this doesn't apply so much to you because you're not in business, or you don't sell for a living. But heed the words of Robert Louis Stevenson: "Everybody lives by selling something."

In *Follow the Yellow Brick Road,* Richard Saul Wurman writes about physicist Isidor Isaac Rabi, who won a Nobel Prize for inventing a technique that permitted scientists to probe the structure of atoms and molecules in the 1930s. Rabi attributed his success in physics to the way his mother used to greet him when he came home from school each day: "Did you ask any good questions today, Isaac?"

By asking questions in your relationships, you are already creating the relationship, and you are already self-motivated. You don't have to wait for the other person to make it happen.

37. Make a relation-shift

Motivate yourself by giving someone *else* the ideas necessary for self-motivation. You can have any experience you want in life simply by giving that experience away to someone else. John Lennon called it "instant karma."

In most of our relationships we stay focused on ourselves. We're fascinated by how we're "coming off." We're constantly monitoring what others must now be thinking of us. We live as if mirrors surround us.

Norman Vincent Peale used to observe that shy people were the greatest egomaniacs on earth, because they were so focused on themselves. You can see that when you observe the body language of a shy person. The looking down and turning in. The curling-up with self-consciousness—as if surrounded by mirrors.

When we shift our focus to the other person in the relationship, something paradoxically powerful happens. By forgetting ourselves we start to grow. I have developed an entire seminar around this one shift. It is called "Relation-Shift."

Spencer Johnson, author of *The One-Minute Sales Person*, calls it "the wonderful paradox: I have more fun, and enjoy more financial success, when I stop trying to get what *I* want and start helping other people get what *they* want."

If you want to be motivated, shift your inspiration to someone else. Point out the strengths of the other individual to him or her. Offer encouragement and support. Offer guidance in his or her own self-motivation. Watch what it does for you.

38. Learn to come from behind

Progress toward your goals is never going to be a straight line. It will always be a bumpy line. You'll go up and then come down a little. Two steps forward and one step back.

There's a good rhythm in that. It is like a dance. There's no rhythm in a straight line upward.

However, people get discouraged when they slide a step back after two steps forward. They think they are failing, and that they've lost it. But they have not. They're simply in step with the natural rhythm of progress. Once you understand this rhythm, you can work with it instead of against it. You can plan the step back.

In *The Power of Optimism,* Alan Loy McGinnis identifies the characteristics of tough-minded optimists, and one of the most important is that optimists always plan for renewal. They know in advance that they are going to run out of energy. "In physics," says McGinnis, "the law of entropy says that all systems, left unattended, will run down. Unless new energy is pumped in, the organism will disintegrate."

Pessimists don't want to plan for renewal, because they don't think there should have to be any. Pessimists are all-or-nothing thinkers. They're always offended when the world is not perfect. They think taking a step backward means something negative about the whole project. "If this were a good marriage, we wouldn't *have* to rekindle the romance," a pessimist would say, dismissing the idea of taking a second honeymoon.

But an optimist knows that there will be ups and downs. And an optimist isn't scared or discouraged by the downs. In fact, an optimist *plans* for the downs, and prepares creative ways to deal with them.

You can schedule your own comebacks. You can look ahead on your calendar and block out time to refresh and renew and recover. Even if you feel very "up" right now, it's smart to plan for renewal. Schedule your own comeback while you're on top. Build in big periods of time to get away—even to get away from what you love.

If you catch yourself thinking that you are too old to do something you want to do, recognize that you are now listening to the pessimistic voice inside of you.

It is not the voice of truth.

You can talk back. You can remind the voice of all the people in life who have started their lives over again at any age they wanted to. John Housman, the Emmy award-winning actor in *The Paper Chase*, started acting professionally when he was in his 70s.

I had a friend named Art Hill, who spent most of his life in advertising. In his heart, however, he always wanted to be a writer. So in his late 50s, he wrote two books that got published by a small publishing house in

Michigan. Then, when he was 60 years old, Hill had his first national release with *I Don't Care if I Never Come Back*, a book about baseball published by Simon and Schuster. The book was a popular and critical success, and his dedication page is something I treasure above any possession I own:

"To Steve Chandler—who cared about writing, cared about me, and one day said, 'You should write a book about baseball.' "

Nobody cares how old you are but you. People only care about what you can do, and you can do anything you want, at any age.

Dr. Monte Buchsbaum of the Mount Sinai School of Medicine in New York has been one of many scientists conducting research into the effects of aging on the brain. He is finding that it isn't aging that causes a brain to become less sharp, it's simply lack of use.

"The good news is that there isn't much difference between a 25-year-old brain and a 75-year-old brain," said Buchsbaum, who used his positron emission tomography laboratory to scan the brains of more than 50 normal volunteers who ranged in age from 20 to 87.

The memory loss and mental passivity that we used to believe was caused by aging has now been proven to be caused by simple lack of use. The brain is like the muscle in your arm: When you use it, it gets strong and quick. When you don't, it grows weak and slow.

Research at the UCLA Brain Research Institute shows that the circuitry of the brain—the dendrites that branch between cells—grows with mental activity.

"Anything that's intellectually challenging," said Arnold Scheibel, head of the Institute, "can probably serve as a kind of stimulus for dendritic growth, which means it adds to the computational reserves in the brain."

Translation: You can make yourself smarter.

"Whoever told you that you cannot increase your intelligence?" asks Dr. Robert Jarvik, inventor of the artificial heart. "Whoever taught you not to try? They didn't know. Flex your mind. Develop it. Use it. It will enrich you and bring you the love of life that thrives on truth and understanding."

Research shows that mathematicians live longer than people in any other profession do, and we never used to know why. Now, in further studies done at UCLA, there has been a direct connection established between dendrite growth and longevity. Mental activity keeps you alive. Lose your mental challenges, and life itself fades away.

Don't listen to the voice inside that talks about your age, or your IQ, or your life history, or anything it can slow you down with. Don't be seduced. You can start a highly motivated life right now by increasing the challenges you give your brain.

39. Come to your own rescue

After a seminar I gave in Vancouver, Canada, Don Beach, the sales manager of Benndorf Verster, one of that city's top businesses, sent me a tape of a song that he wanted me to hear.

He said it reminded him of what I had been teaching his team about self-esteem. The song was a live performance by the old folk-singing duo, Sonny Terry and Brownie McGee. The song is called "Love, Truth and Confidence." It's about how we foolishly chase after love and try to discover the ultimate truth, while ignoring something much more vital to our happiness: confidence.

The chorus of the song goes like this: *"Love and truth / you can find / any place, anywhere, any time / but you can just say 'so long' / once confidence is gone / nothing matters anymore."*

I never knew the true power of self-confidence until I began working with Dr. Nathaniel Branden and his wife Devers Branden. Both are authors and psychotherapists with the Branden Institute for Self-Esteem, and they have provided me with the most powerful insights I've ever received into how I operate as a human being.

Dr. Branden's book, *The Six Pillars of Self-Esteem,* is unlike any other psychology book on the market, because in addition to its eloquently written philosophy on how to build inner strength, it also contains a full year's worth of practical, powerful, user-friendly exercises to raise your own consciousness and self-esteem. His sentence-completion exercises are so effective and exciting that if you do them, I can say without a trace of exaggeration, you can get tens of thousands of dollars worth of personal growth therapy for the price of a single book.

Before you assume that Branden's notion of self-esteem is the same as that being bandied about by New-Age educators, you must read his work and listen to his tapes. Most people today think others can bestow self-esteem on us. Such misguided thinking leads to phenomena such as classes without grades and work without standards for excellence. Perhaps you have heard about that Little League group in Pennsylvania that wanted to eliminate keeping score from baseball games because of the damage that losing does to children's self-esteem.

When we confuse pampering and coddling with instilling self-esteem, we really encourage the upbringing of young, sensitive children who have no inner strength whatsoever. When it comes time for such overpraised, underachieving kids to find success in the competitive global marketplace, they will be confused, fearful, and ineffective.

The concepts taught by Nathaniel and Devers Branden are intellectually ruthless and unsentimental. Some of the best ideas go all the way back to Branden's years working with the great novelist and objectivist philosopher Ayn Rand.

The Brandens have taught me how to objectively explore the weaknesses in my own thinking and to challenge the self-deception that was undermining my effectiveness in life.

"To trust one's mind and to know that one is worthy of happiness is the essence of self-esteem," writes Dr. Branden. "The value of self-esteem lies not merely in the fact that it allows us to *feel* better, but that it allows us to *live* better—to respond to challenges and opportunities more resourcefully and appropriately."

The two ideas contained in the Brandens' work that have most helped me are: 1) "You can't leave a place you've never been"; and 2) "No one is coming."

I used to believe that I could *run* from all my frightening thoughts and beliefs about myself. But all that ever did was create deeper internal fears and conflicts. What I really needed was to get all my fears into the sunshine and demystify them. Once I systematically began to do that, I was able to dismantle those fears, as a bomb squad dismantles a bomb.

Acceptance and full consciousness of those fears—and the self-sabotaging behavior they led to—was "the place I had never been." Once I was in that place, I could leave.

The notion that "no one is coming" was somehow terrifying to accept. The idea that no one was going to res-
cue me from my circumstances is an idea that I might
never have accepted. That idea sounded too much like
the final abandonment. It contradicted all my childhood
self-programming. (Many of us, even as grown-ups, devise very elaborate and subtle variations on the "I want
my mommy" theme.) The Brandens showed me that I
could be much happier and more effective if I valued
independence and self-responsibility above dependency
on someone else.

When you accept the idea that "no one is coming" it
is actually a very powerful moment, because it means
that *you* are enough. No one needs to come. You can
handle your problems yourself. You are, in a larger
sense, appropriate to life. You can grow and get strong
and generate your own happiness.

And paradoxically, from that position of independence, truly great relationships can be built, because
they aren't based on dependency and fear. They are
based on mutual independence and love.

Once, in a group therapy session, a client of Dr.
Branden's challenged him on his principle that "no one
is coming." "But Nathaniel," the client said, "it's not true.
You came!"

"Correct," admitted Dr. Branden, "but I came to say
that no one is coming."

40. Find your soul purpose

How do you know what your true life is? Or what
your soul's purpose is? How do you know how to live
this purpose? The answers to these questions are yours
for the taking, but you must *seize* the answers and not
wait to be given them. No one will give you the answers.

One good clue as to whether you are living your true life is how much you fear death. Do you fear death a lot, just a little, or not at all?

"When you say you fear death," wrote David Viscott, "you are really saying that you fear you have not lived your true life. This fear cloaks the world in silent suffering."

When mythologist Joseph Campbell recommended that we "follow our bliss," many people misunderstood him. They thought he meant to become a pleasure-seeker, a selfish hedonist from the "me generation." Instead, he meant that in order to find out what your true life could be, you should look for clues in whatever makes you happy.

What gets you excited? In the answer to that question, you'll discover where you can be of most service. You can't live your true life if you're not serving people, and you can't serve people very well if you are not excited about what you're doing.

What makes you happy? (I know I already asked, but the fear that "cloaks the world in silent suffering" comes from *not* asking that question enough times.)

In my own professional life I have finally found that teaching makes me happy, writing makes me happy, and performing makes me happy. It took me many years of unhappiness to finally reach the point of despair necessary to ask the question: What makes me happy?

I was the creative director for an ad agency and I was making a good deal of money producing commercials, meeting with clients, and designing marketing strategies. I could have done this type of work forever, but my horrible fear of death was my clue that I was not living my true life.

"People living deeply," wrote Anaïs Nin, "have no fear of death." I was not living deeply. And it took me a long time to get clear answers to my question: What makes me happy? But any question we ask ourselves often enough will eventually yield the right answer. The problem is, we quit asking.

Fortunately for me, in this rare instance of persistence in the face of extreme discomfort, I didn't quit asking. The answer came to me in the form of a memory—so colorful it was almost like a movie scene. I was driving at night in my car 10 years earlier, and I was as happy as I had ever been. In fact, I was driving around aimlessly so that I could keep my feeling of happiness preserved and contained within that car—I didn't want anything to interrupt it. It was so profound that it lasted for hours.

The occasion had been a speech I had just given. The subject of it was my recovery from an addiction, and the night that I spoke I was running such a high fever, and I had such a fear of speaking in public that I tried to call the talk off. My hosts wouldn't hear of it.

Somehow I made it to the podium and, probably because my fever and flu were so intense, I spoke freely, without caution or self-consciousness. The more I spoke about freedom from addiction, the more excited I got. My creativity just soared. I remember the audience laughing as I spoke. I remember them jumping to their feet and cheering when I was finished. It was the most remarkable night of my life. Somehow I had reached people in a way I'd never reached people before, and their own expressions of joy lifted me higher than I had ever been.

It was that memory of that moonlit night, driving in my car, that came back to me 10 years later after I'd spent weeks repeating to myself the question, "What makes me happy?" Now I had the picture, but I had no idea how to act on it. But at least I knew what my true life was, and I knew that I wasn't living it.

Then one day one of my major advertising clients asked me to hire a motivational speaker for a big breakfast meeting they were having for their sales staff. I didn't know of anyone in Arizona who was any good—the only motivational speakers I was familiar with were the national ones whose tapes I'd listened to so often in my car, people such as Wayne Dyer, Tom Peters, Anthony Robbins, Alan Watts, and Nathaniel Branden. But Alan Watts was dead—and the rest were probably far too expensive for our little breakfast.

So I called Kirk Nelson, a friend of mine who was sales manager at KTAR in Phoenix, and asked his advice. "The only person in Arizona worth hiring is Dennis Deaton," he said. "He speaks all over the country, and he's usually booked, but if you can get him, do, because he's great."

I finally reached Deaton in Utah, where he was giving seminars on time management. He agreed to come back to Phoenix in time for our breakfast and give a 45-minute motivational talk.

Kirk Nelson was right. Deaton was impressive. He held the audience spellbound as he told stories that illustrated his ideas about the power that people have over their thoughts, and the mastery that they can achieve over their thinking. When he finished speaking and came back to the table where we had been sitting, I shook his hand and thanked him, and I found myself making a silent vow that someday soon I would be working with this man.

It wasn't long after that that he and I were indeed working together. It was at a company called Quma

Learning, Deaton's corporate training facility based in Phoenix, Arizona. Although I began with Quma as its marketing director—creating advertisements, video scripts, and direct-mail pieces—I soon worked my way up to the position of seminar presenter.

My first big thrill came when Deaton and I were both invited to speak at a national convention of carpet-cleaning companies. It was the first time I had ever shared the stage with him, and I was to go on first. He was in the audience when I spoke, and I have to admit I had worked harder than I'd ever worked in my life in preparation for this event.

The participants had heard Deaton before at previous conventions and loved him, but they'd never heard me. After my presentation was over, they clapped enthusiastically and as Deaton passed me on his way to the stage he was beaming with pride as he shook my hand. (Unlike myself, Dennis Deaton has very little professional jealousy of other speakers. He was happy for my success. I have to admit that my favorite moment occurred when, after he was introduced, someone in the audience teasingly shouted out, "Dennis who?")

Many people get confused and believe that living their true life means getting lucky and finding a suitable job with an appreciative boss somewhere. What I have come to realize is that you can live your true life anywhere, in any job, with any boss.

First find out what makes you happy, and then start doing it. If writing makes you happy, and you're not writing for a living, start up a company newsletter or your own Web site. When I first realized that speaking and teaching made me happy, I started a free weekly workshop. I didn't wait until something was offered to me.

Whatever goal you want to reach, you can reach it 10 times faster if you are happy. In my sales training and consulting, I notice that happy salespeople sell at least twice as much as unhappy salespeople. Most people think that the successful salespeople are happy because they are selling more and making more money. Not true. They are selling more and making more money *because they are happy*.

As J.D. Salinger's character Seymour says in *Franny and Zooey*, "This happiness is strong stuff!" Happiness is the strongest stuff in the world. It is more energizing than a cup of hot espresso on a cold morning. It is more mind-expanding than a dose of acid. It is more intoxicating than a glass of champagne under the stars.

If you refuse to cultivate happiness in yourself, you will not be of extraordinary service to others, and you will not have the energy to create who you want to be. There is no goal better than this one: to know as you lie on your deathbed that you lived your true life because you did what made you happy.

41. Get up on the right side

Since I was a child, I've always been intrigued with the idea that you could have a great day just by getting up on the right side of the bed. Later in life, during my years as a largely unsuccessful songwriter, one of the few successes I had was with a country rock song that I co-wrote with Fred Knipe and Duncan Stitt. It was called "The Right Side of the Wrong Bed."

Today my fascination is not so much with the right side of the bed as it is with the right side of the *head*— or to be more precise, the right side of the brain.

In the 1930s, brain surgeons discovered the different functions of the two halves of the brain while working with epileptics. In 1950, Roger W. Sperry of the University of Chicago (and later of Cal Tech) made the greatest breakthroughs in discovering that dreams, energy, and creative insight come from the right side of the brain, while linear, logical, short-term, and short-sighted thinking come from the left.

The best explanation of how "whole-brain" thinking surpasses left-brain thinking or right-brain thinking is in a book written by British philosopher Colin Wilson called *Frankenstein's Castle*. Wilson reveals that we have more control over drawing vital energy and creative ideas from the "right brain" than we ever realized. And what stimulates the right brain the most is a high sense of purpose.

If you had to carry a heavy sack of sand across town, your left brain might get upset and tell you that you were doing something boring and tedious. However, if your child were injured badly and she weighed the same as the huge bag of sand, you'd carry her the same distance to the hospital with a surprising surge of vital energy (sent from the right brain). That's what purpose does to the brain. Self-motivation gets more and more exciting as the left brain gets better and better at telling the right brain what to do.

42. Let your whole brain play

Suicide rates go down during times of war because many people begin to feel useful and challenged enough times during the day. This encourages them to us both sides of the brain harmonically. In less eventful times, people tend to slip into using just one side of the brain and get trapped into feeling useless.

Most people unconsciously wait for an external crisis, such as a threatened bankruptcy or an attack on the street or the burning down of their home or an unwanted divorce, or a war, to kick in their whole-brain thinking.

But that passive misuse of the brain leads to a life of reaction rather than creation. When Oliver Wendell Holmes said "most people go to their graves with their music still in them," he just as easily could have said that most people live in their left brain only. When Thoreau said "most men lead lives of quiet desperation," he was describing what life is like if you stay trapped in left, linear, short-sighted thinking.

But the irony is that the left brain has gotten an unfairly negative reputation, simply because people stay trapped there. When people learn that the left brain is there to connect with the right, then it takes on new power and function. When people stay trapped in linear, flat, and logical left-brain thinking and never activate the creative right side of the brain, they lose their love of life. The right brain comes alive during dreaming at night while the left brain sleeps. But it is possible (as artists, poets, and saints can attest) to have the same two-sided interplay that we had as children, while we are awake. We simply have to fire it up by using the left brain to call on the right. This is what happens when we make love, play games, write poetry, hold a baby, or face a threatening crisis: The left brain commands the right brain to come alive and get involved. That is when you get whole-brain thinking, or what psychologist Abraham Maslow called "peak" experiences.

The three best ways to activate whole-brain thinking are through 1) goal-visualization, 2) joyful work, and 3) revitalizing play. Rather than wait for external crises to appear, _create_ internal challenge games of your own—goals and purposes—that lead you in growth toward the motivated person you want to become.

The real excitement in studies of the power of the right brain lies in its suggestion of a neurological basis for personal transformation. It's not just motivational puff or secular evangelism to say that we possess unlimited creative energy, and we can use it to create the lives we want.

"In fact," writes Colin Wilson, "we can learn to live on a far, far higher level of power. And that is what the left brain was intended for. Its farsightedness gives it the ability to summon power. Yet it hardly makes use of this ability. It could be compared to a man who possesses a magic machine that will create gold coins so that he could, if he wanted, pay off the national debt and abolish poverty. But he is so lazy and stupid that he never bothers to make more than a couple of coins every day—just enough to see him through until the evening...or perhaps he is not lazy: only afraid of emptying the machine. If so, the fear is unnecessary. It is magical, and cannot be emptied."

Most people regard their right brain with a sense of wonder. They think inspiring thoughts "came to them" out of the blue. "Last night I had the strangest dream!" they will say, not knowing how much control they really have over that magical machine.

43. Get your stars out

Terry Hill is a writer who has lived all over the world and has been a friend of mine since we met each other in the sixth grade in Birmingham, Michigan. His short story, "Cafes Are for Handicapping," features an intriguing character named Joe Warner who liked to tell stories about horse racing.

Joe Warner told the story of being in the press box at Belmont when Secretariat put away the Triple Crown by 31 lengths.

"And I looked beside me when he was coming down the stretch at all these hardened, cigar-chomping New York newspapermen and they all had tears running down their cheeks like little babies. 'Course I couldn't see too clear myself for the tears in my eyes. I was 23 at the time. And it was the first Triple Crown in my lifetime. Imagine that."

That story brought me even closer to a question I've been asking all my life. Why do we cry when we see huge accomplishments? Why do we cry at weddings? Why do I cry when the blind girl jumps with her horse in the movie *Wild Hearts Can't Be Broken*? Or when the Titans win the game in Denzel Washington's *Remember the Titans*? Why did those sportswriters cry to see that horse win by 31 lengths?

This is my theory: We weep for the winner inside of all of us. In these poignant moments, we cry because we know for a fact that there is something in us that could be every bit as great as what we are watching. We are, for that moment, the untapped greatness we are seeing. But we get tears in our eyes, because we know the greatness isn't being realized. We could have been like that, but we aren't.

Terry Hill also gives public talks on creativity. His own work in advertising and public relations throughout the years has won countless awards and, as one might expect, he presents some learned and sophisticated formulae for "creating." But he finishes all his talks by saying it is really a simple thing to be creative—all you do is "get your stars out." That's how you tap into the untapped you.

His reference is to *Seymour: An Introduction* by J.D. Salinger. Seymour is writing a letter to his brother Buddy, who has chosen to become a professional writer. Seymour tells his brother that writing has always been more than a profession, that it has been more like Buddy's religion. He says that Buddy will be asked two very profound questions when he dies about the writing he was doing: 1) "Were most of your stars out?"; and 2) "Were you busy writing your heart out?"

Terry Hill's advice to his audiences on the subject of creativity is to make sure you "get your stars out." This is another way of saying let the stars that are in you shine freely. Don't force them out. Just let them shine.

Although Hill's audiences are usually advertising people and writers, his recommendations apply to all of us. Our lives are ours to create. Do we want to create them in a lackluster way or do we want to be inspiring? When we write our plans and dreams, we need to write our hearts out. In shooting for the stars, it's time to get a bit wild. Wild hearts can't be broken.

44. Just make everything up

Sometimes in my seminars I will ask the people in the audience to raise their hands if they think of themselves as "creative." I've never had more than a fourth of the audience raise their hands.

I then ask the people how many of them were able to make things up when they were younger—make up names for their dolls, make up a game to play, make up a story for their parents when the truth looked less promising.

All hands go up.

So, what's the difference? You made stuff up as a child, but you're not a creative adult? The difference is that we have charged the word "creative" with meaning something truly extraordinary. Picasso was creative. Meryl Streep is creative. Wyclef Jean is creative. But me?

So one of the ways to get started creating goals and action plans is to just "make them up," like you did as a kid. Think of creating in simpler terms. Think of it as something all humans do very easily. French psychologist Emile Coue said, "Always think of what you have to do as easy and it will be."

45. Put on your game face

I used to hate to study for tests in high school. Nothing could have been more boring. But one day Terry Hill and I decided to make a game of it. We decided to challenge each other by making up mock tests for each other. The only rules were that we had to ask 30 questions, and the answers had to appear in the text that we were going to be tested on in the classroom the next day.

Because we were both competitive and loved games, we worked very hard to come up with the most ridiculously difficult questions we could devise. "What was Magellan's middle name?" "How many of Custer's children were daughters?" "What is the 23rd word in the Gettysburg Address?" We also tried to anticipate the other's toughest questions and learn the obscure answers.

On the morning of the real test we presented each other with our own tests, *always* twice as hard as the real test. As we each took each other's test there was much happy yelling and laughter. But by the time we took the real test in school, we were more than ready. In fact, we often looked across the classroom at each other during the real test and rolled our eyes with disdain at the simplicity and stupidity of the real exam.

By changing our study into a challenging game, we had taken the "work" out of the task and replaced it with play. Did we work as hard? Harder! But by transforming work into play, we increased our energy and our sense of creativity.

Most people who play a lot of golf or tennis work much harder at their games than they do at work. All people work harder at play than they do at work, because there's no resistance. Golfers are working harder on the golf course than they are at their professions. They don't always know this (although their spouses usually do) because it doesn't feel like work—it feels like fun. They bring more energy, innovation, and zest to what they're doing out on the course *because* it's a game. They also bring an ongoing commitment to increasing their skills. Everyone is interested in getting better at the games they play.

As for the effect of games on energy, consider a bunch of guys playing poker all night. Because poker is a game, people can play it all night until the sun comes up. When they finally come home to sleep, you might be tempted to ask them, "How did you manage to stay up all night? Were you drinking coffee and cokes?" No, they confess, they were drinking beer. "But shouldn't beer slow you down and make you tired?" Not if you are playing a game! In fact, you'll also learn that they were probably smoking cigars and eating junk snacks as well. Not generally known as stimulants. What *was* stimulating was the game. The joy of competition.

Playwright Noel Coward once said, "Work is more fun than fun." I included that quote in a seminar guidebook for a sales group a year ago and one of the participants in the back of the room raised his hand and said, "Yeah, Steve, who is this Noel Coward guy? I figure with a quote like that he's either a porn star or a professional golfer."

That line got a great laugh at my expense, but it also revealed a truth (which almost all humor does). People believe that the *fun* jobs are always somewhere else. "If only I could get a job like that!" "If only I had been a pro golfer." But the truth is that fulfilling and fun work can be found in anything. The more we consciously introduce game-playing elements (personal bests listed, goals, time limits, competition with self or others, record-keeping, etc.) the more fun the activity becomes.

I recently worked on a project with a young man in Phoenix who was selling three times as much office equipment as the average salesperson on his team. He said he didn't understand his co-workers who got depressed easily, took rejection hard, and struggled with putting their deals together.

"I don't take this that seriously," he smiled. "I love all my sales challenges. The tougher the prospect is, the more fun I have selling. There is absolutely nothing personal or depressing in any of this for me. When I meet a new sales prospect, it's a chess game."

Whatever it is you have to do, whether it's a major project at work, or a huge cleaning job at home, turning it into a *game* will always bring you higher levels of energy and motivation.

46. Discover active relaxation

There is a huge difference between active relaxation and passive relaxation. When we play video games, play computer games, play cards, work in the garden, walk the dog, go into a chat room, or play chess, we are interacting with the unexpected, and our minds are responding. All of these activities increase personal creativity and intellectual motivation. They are all active pursuits.

Active relaxation refreshes and restores the mind. It keeps it flexible and toned for thinking. Great thinkers have known this secret for a long time. Winston Churchill used to paint to relax. Albert Einstein played the violin. They could relax one part of the brain while stimulating another. When they returned to workday pursuits they were fresher and sharper than ever.

Most of us try to deaden the mind in order to relax. We rent mindless videos, read pulp fiction, drink, smoke, and eat until we're foggy and bloated. The problem with this form of relaxation is that it dulls our spirit and makes it hard to come back to consciousness.

I accidentally discovered the restorative powers of video and computer games when I played some with my then-9-year-old son Bobby. What began as a way to make him happy and spend time with him became a brain-challenging pursuit. The complexity of computer football, basketball, and hockey games now rivals chess and *The New York Times* Sunday crossword puzzle. It requires stimulating recreational thinking.

"Thinking is the hardest work we do," said Henry Ford, "which is why so few people ever do it." But when we find ways to link thinking to recreation, our lives get richer. We become players in the game of life and not just spectators.

47. Make today a masterpiece

Most of us think our lives accumulate. We think they are adding up to something. We think of our lives as being strung together like a long smoky train, so that we can add new freight cars when we're feeling right, and dump the others on a siding somewhere when we're not.

But when basketball legend John Wooden's father said to him, "Make each day your masterpiece," Wooden knew something profound: Life is *now*. Life is not later on. And the more we hypnotize ourselves into thinking we have all the time in the world to do what we want to do, the more we sleepwalk past life's finest opportunities. Self-motivation flows from the importance we attach to *today*.

John Wooden was the most successful college basketball coach of all time. His UCLA teams won 10 national championships in a 12-year time span. Wooden created a major portion of his coaching and living philosophy from one thought—a single sentence passed on to him by his father when Wooden was a little boy— "Make each day your masterpiece."

While other coaches would try to gear their players toward important games in the future, Wooden always focused on *today*. His practice sessions at UCLA were every bit as important as any championship game. In his philosophy, there was no reason not to make today the proudest day of your life. There was no reason not to play as hard in practice as you do in a game. He wanted every player to go to bed each night thinking, "Today I was at my best."

Most of us, however, don't want it to be this way. If someone asks us if today can be used as a model to judge our entire life by, we would shriek, "On no! It isn't one of my better days. Give me a year or two and I'll live a day, I'm certain of it, that you can use to represent my life."

The key to personal transformation is in your willingness to do very tiny things—but to do them *today*.

Transformation is not an all-or-nothing game, it's a work in progress. A little touch here and a small touch there is what makes your day (and, therefore, your life) great. Today is a microcosm of your entire life. It is your whole life in miniature. You were "born" when you woke up, and you'll "die" when you go to sleep. It was designed this way, so that you could live your whole life in a day.

48. Enjoy all your problems

Every solution has a problem.

You can't have one without the other. So why do we say that we hate problems? Why do we claim to want a hassle-free existence? When someone is emotionally sick, why do we say, "He's got problems"?

Deep down, where our wisdom lives, we know that problems are good for us. When my daughter's teacher talks to me during open house and tells me that my daughter is going to be "working more problems" in math than she worked last year, I think that's wonderful. Why do I think it's wonderful when my daughter gets more problems to solve, if I think problems are a problem?

Because somehow we know that problems are good for our children. By solving problems, our kids will become more self-sufficient. They'll trust their own minds more. They'll see themselves as problem-*solvers*.

Because we ourselves are so superstitious about our own problems, we tend to run from them rather than solve them. We have demonized problems to such a degree that they are like monsters that live under the bed. And by not solving them during the day, we tremble over them at night.

When people took their problems to the legendary insurance giant W. Clement Stone, he used to shout out, "You've got a problem? That's great!" It's a wonder he wasn't shot by someone, given our culture's deep superstition about problems.

But problems are not to be feared. Problems are not curses. Problems are simply tough games for the athletes of the mind and true athletes always long to get a game going.

In *The Road Less Traveled*, one of M. Scott Peck's central themes is that "problems call forth our wisdom and our courage."

One of the best ways to approach a problem is in a spirit of play, the same way you approach a chess game or a challenge to play one-on-one playground basketball. One of my favorite ways to play with a problem, especially one that seems hopeless, is to ask myself, "What is a funny way to solve this problem? What would be a hilarious solution?" That question never fails to open up fresh new avenues of thought.

"Every problem in your life," said Richard Bach, author of *Illusions*, "carries a gift inside it." He is right. But we have to be thinking that way first, or the gift will never appear.

In his groundbreaking studies of natural healing, Dr. Andrew Weil suggests that we even regard illness as a gift. "Because illness can be such a powerful stimulus to change," he writes in *Spontaneous Healing*, "perhaps it is the only thing that can force some people to resolve their deepest conflicts. Successful patients often come to regard it as the greatest opportunity they ever had for personal growth and development—truly a gift. Seeing illness as a misfortune, especially one that is undeserved, may obstruct the healing system. Coming to see the illness as a gift that allows you to grow may unlock it."

If you see your problems as curses, the motivation you're looking for in life will be hard to find. If you learn to love the opportunities your problems present, then your motivational energy will rise.

49. Remind your mind

Perhaps you have noted an idea in this book, or another recent book that you've read, that you want to hold on to. It might be an idea that you knew, the moment you saw it, would always be useful to you. You might even have underlined it for future reference.

But what if the book goes on the shelf, or gets loaned to a friend, and is forevermore out of sight and out of mind? This is a very common experience, and there is a remedy: Start treating self-motivational ideas as if they were songs.

You can find ways to rewind these ideas so they'll play again and again until you can't get them out of your head. That's how belief systems are restructured to suit our goals. Place the thought you want to remember into the jingle track in your brain so that it can't get out.

You can create a new self by learning the beliefs you want to live by—one thought at a time. Learn these thoughts as you would the lyrics for a song you had to perform on stage. A friend of mine used to learn his parts in musicals by placing index cards with song lyrics all over his office, home, and bathroom mirror. He sometimes had them on the dashboard of his car. Why? He was making a conscious visual effort to reach the backside of his own mind.

The trick is to keep this motivation going. To deliberately feed your spirit with the optimistic ideas you want to live by. Any time a thought, sentence, or paragraph inspires you or opens up your thinking, you need to capture it, like a butterfly in a net, and later release it into your own field of consciousness.

For me, discovering an exciting idea in a book or magazine is like a true peak experience. It makes the world bright and incomprehensible. I get that tingle in my spine. I get that "Oh, yes!" feeling. Why am I this lucky? And the more I deliberately fill my mind with the words and phrases that originally stirred the peak experience, the easier it is to remember that life is good.

"This," writes Colin Wilson in _New Pathways in Psychology,_ "is why people who have a peak experience can go on repeating them: because it is simply a matter of _reminding yourself_ of something you have already seen and which you know to be real. In this sense, it is like any other 'recognition' that suddenly dawns on you—for example, the recognition of the greatness of some composer or artist whom you had formerly found difficult or incomprehensible, or the recognition of how to solve a certain problem. Once such a recognition 'dawns' it is easy to reestablish contact with it, because it is there like some possession, waiting for you to return to it."

During my talks on self-motivation, one of the questions I'm asked most often is "How do I keep this going?" People say, "I love what I've learned today, but I've often gone to seminars that got me motivated and then a few days later I was back to my old pessimistic self, doing exactly what I used to do."

If I were in the mood to be blunt, I would answer the question this way: Why, if you love what you've learned about self-motivation, would you ask *me* how to keep it going in your life? The person in this room best equipped to answer your question is you. So I'll ask you, "How will you keep this going in your life?" I bet you could give me 10 ways you could do it. And I bet that if this were a foreign language you had to learn you would set aside a certain amount of time each day to review it, to read it out loud, and to make certain you learned it. I bet you'd buy tapes or CDs for your car and even arrange small study groups. So the real question is this: Is mastering the art of motivation as important as learning another language?

Even a single phrase, placed prominently in a home or office, can have a huge impact on your life. In Arnold Schwarzenegger's childhood home in a poor town in Austria, his father framed and hung the simple words, "Joy Through Strength." It's not hard to see what effect that idea had on Arnold's life.

Once while I was attending a Werner Erhard seminar, I had some free time during a break so I wrote myself a letter. I put down all the ideas I wanted to remember from the seminar and I sealed them in an envelope. I took it home and a month later I mailed it to myself. When I opened it at work and read it, it was like a fresh experience all over again.

I was so impressed by how effective this was for me that I employed the idea in one of my own seminars. I had everyone in the audience write out the important insights they'd received and what they intended to do differently in their lives from this moment on. When the people were finished, I asked them to seal the letters into the envelopes I'd provided and address the envelopes to *themselves*. I told them I would hold them for a month and then mail them all.

The reports I got back were remarkable. Some people said seeing those thoughts written to themselves in their own handwriting brought the whole seminar back to them. They felt a rush of excitement and a new commitment to take action.

Are you willing to remind yourself to treat yourself to your own best thoughts? Are you willing to set visual traps and ambushes, so you'll always see words and thoughts you know you want to remember?

50. Get down and get small

The fewer goals you set each day, the more you feel "pushed around" by people and events that are beyond your control.

You suffer from a sense of powerlessness. Rather than creating the reality you want, you are only reacting to the world around you. You have much more control over the activities of your day than you realize.

By increasing your conscious use of small objectives, you will see the larger objectives coming into reality.

Most people participating in the free enterprise system have become thoroughly convinced of the power of setting large and specific long-range goals for themselves. Career goals, yearly goals, and monthly performance goals are always on the mind of a person with ambition.

But often those people overlook altogether the power of small goals—goals set during the day that give energy to the day and a sense of achieving a lot of small "wins" along the way.

In his psychological masterpiece, _Flow: The Psychology of Optimal Experience,_ Mihaly Csikszentmihalyi refers to large goals as "outcome" goals and small goals as "process" goals. The beauty of "process" goals is that they are always within your immediate power to achieve. For example, you might set a process goal of making four important telephone calls before lunch. On a sheet of paper you make four boxes, and as you make each call you fill in a box, and when the four are made, you file the paper in your goal folder and go enjoy lunch. Because you've earned it.

You can set process goals, for example, before a conversation with a person. I want to find these three things out, I want to ask these four questions, I want to make these two requests, and I want to pay my client one compliment before I leave.

Process goals give you total focus. When you are constantly setting process goals, you are in more control of your day, and you feel a sense of skillful self-motivation.

At the end of the day, or the beginning of the next day, you can check your progress toward your "outcome" goals. You can adjust your process goals to take you closer to the outcomes you want, and always keep the two in harmony.

Let's say it's now the end of a long, hard day. You have a half hour before you have to go home. If you're not in the habit of setting process goals, you might say, "I guess I ought to do some paperwork or make a call or two before I go home." You look at the pile of paper on your desk, or you mindlessly thumb through phone numbers, and all of a sudden someone comes by your desk to chat. Because *you have nothing specific to do* you engage in conversation and, before you know it, the half hour is gone and you have to go home. Even though you didn't leave anything specific unfinished, you still have that vague feeling of having wasted time.

Now what happens if you use that half hour to set and achieve a process goal? "Before I go home tonight I'm going to send out two good letters of introduction with all my marketing material included." Now you have a process goal and only a half hour in which to do it.

When the person comes by your desk to chat, you tell him you'll have to talk to him later because you've got some things "that have to get out" by five.

People who get into the swing of setting small goals all day long report a much higher level of consciousness and energy. It's as if they are athletes constantly coaching themselves through an ongoing game. They are happier people because their day is being created by the power inside their own minds, and *not* by the power of the world around them.

51. Advertise to yourself

I often start the day by drawing four circles on a blank piece of paper.

The circles represent my day (today), my month, my year, and my life. Inside each circle I write down what I want. It can be a dollar figure, it can be anything, and the goals can change from day to day—it doesn't matter. There is no way to get this process "wrong."

But by writing the goals down, I am like an airline pilot who is consulting his or her map prior to takeoff. I am orienting my mind to what I am up to in life. I am *reminding* myself of what I really want. We wouldn't think, before an airline flight, of poking our heads into the cabin and saying to the pilot, "Just take me anywhere!" Yet that's how we live our days when we don't check the map.

Sometimes in my seminars on motivation, people observe that they "don't have time" for goal setting. But the four-circle system I described takes only four minutes!

Once during a workshop on goal setting, I asked if anyone in the audience had any interesting experiences with visualization. We had been discussing sports psychologist Rob Gilbert's observation that "losers visualize the penalties of failure, and winners visualize the rewards of success."

A young couple shared a story about how they had wanted for years to buy their own home but never got the money together to do it. Then one day, after reading about the practice of "treasure-mapping" (posting pictures of what you want in life somewhere in your office or home), they decided to put a picture on their refrigerator of a new house, the kind they dreamed of owning.

"In less than nine months, we'd made the down payment and moved in," said the amazed husband. His wife added, "Alongside the photo of the house we eventually put a little thermometer that we filled in as our savings toward a down payment grew."

I have heard many similar stories about how treasure-mapping has worked for people. I have also read books and attended seminars that explain why. Most of them discuss what happens to the subconscious mind when you send it a picture of something you want. Because the subconscious mind only communicates with vividly imagined or real pictures, it will not seek to bring into your life anything you can't picture.

Without advertising our goals to ourselves, we can lose sight of them altogether. It is possible to go an entire week, or two or three, without thinking about our main goals in life. We get caught up in reacting and responding to people and circumstances and we simply forget to think about our own purpose.

I have an example of how this practice worked in my life: Three years ago I was interested in giving more seminars on the subject of fund-raising. I had co-authored a book called *RelationSHIFT: Revolutionary Fund-Raising* with University of Arizona development director Michael Bassoff. We had done some successful seminars on the subject, and I wanted to do more. So, on the wall of my bedroom I put up a white poster board, and on that board I put up a lot of pictures and index cards with my goals on them. I wanted to have all those goals in front of me when I woke up each morning, even though I only spent a minute or two looking at the board each day.

One of the index cards I had pinned to my goal board simply contained the bold-markered letters, "ASU." It was almost lost among the hodgepodge of photos and goals I'd covered the board with, and I'm certain I only barely noticed it each morning as I got up. I put it up there because I thought it would be great if I could give seminars to Arizona State University, especially now that I was living in the Phoenix area. I really thought nothing more of it.

One day at the offices of the corporate training company where I worked, I was asked to shake the hand of a new employee, Jerry. I asked Jerry to come in and sit down. We talked in my office for a few minutes about his joining the company. I asked him about his family and he casually mentioned that his parents were living in town, and that his mother worked at ASU.

Normally, that would have meant nothing. ASU is a very well-known and oft-mentioned presence in the Phoenix area. But something went off in my mind when he said that, and I know in hindsight that "something" was my daily view of my goal board.

My ears perked up when he said "ASU" and I asked him, "What does your mother do at ASU?" "She's the chief administrative assistant to the development director at the ASU Foundation," he said. "They're in charge of all the fund-raising at the University."

I really brightened at that point, and I told Jerry about my past work in fund-raising at the University of Arizona in Tucson, and how I'd always wanted to do similar work at ASU. He said he'd be delighted to introduce me to his mother and to the development director himself.

Within a month, ASU fund-raisers were attending my seminar in *"RelationSHIFT"* and I had realized one of the goals on my board.

I honestly believe that if I had not had a goal board up in my bedroom, Jerry's mention of ASU would have gone right past me.

And this illustrates something important. We need to advertise our own goals to ourselves. Otherwise, our psychic energy is spread too thin across the spectrum of things that aren't that important to us.

52. Think outside the box

Once I attended a new business proposal presentation by Bob Koether, in which he had his prospective customers all play a little nine-dot game that illustrated to them that the solutions to puzzles are often simple to see if we think in unconventional ways.

As people laughed and tore up their puzzles in frustration when Koether showed them the solution, he stood up to make his final point.

"We restrict our thinking for no good reason," said Koether. "We do things simply because that's the way we always did them. I want you to know that our commitment in serving your company is to *always look outside the box* for the most innovative solutions possible to our problems. We'll never do something just because that's the way we have always done it"

To many business leaders pitching a lucrative account, this kind of puzzle-solving exercise would simply be considered a clever presentation. But to Bob Koether, it was a symbolic expression of his whole life in business.

Once, on a Xerox-sponsored trip in Cancun, Mexico, Bob and Mike spent the day out in treacherous waters on a fishing boat. After coming ashore, they retired to Carlos O'Brien's restaurant for tequila and beer and a period of reflection on their lives in sales thus far.

"We knew that as well as we had done, we would never own boats like the one we were just in if we remained at Xerox," said Bob. "We talked about possibilities in the bar, and it wasn't long before we noticed some black T-shirts on the wall with the word *infinity* on them. Then, for more than two hours, Mike and I discussed just what the word *infinity* meant. Out of that discussion, a dream was born, a dream that took shape in the form of Infinity Communications."

Bob Koether and his brother believed that there was one vital area in which Xerox was underperforming—and that was customer service. What if, they asked, a company's commitment to the customer was infinite? Not boxed-in, but unlimited in its possibilities for creative service?

With that concept as motivation, the two brothers formed "Infincom" (short for Infinity Communications) in the state of Arizona, and within 10 years they grew from six employees and no customers into a $50 million business with more than 500 employees. And for the past three years straight, the *Arizona Business Gazette* has ranked Infincom the number-one office equipment company in Arizona—ahead of Xerox.

All of us tend to look at our challenges from inside a box. We take what we've done in the past and put it in front of our eyes and then try to envision what we call "the future." But that restricts our future. With that restricted view, the best the future can be is a "new and better past."

Great motivational energy occurs when we get out of the box and assume that the possibilities for creative ideas are infinite. To realize the best possible future for yourself, don't look at it through a box containing your own past.

53. Keep thinking, keep thinking

Motivation comes from thought.

Every act we take is preceded by a thought that inspires that act. And when we quit thinking, we lose the motivation to act. We eventually slip into pessimism, and the pessimism leads to even *less* thinking. And so it goes. A downward spiral of negativity and passivity, feeding on itself like cancer.

I like to use this example in my seminars to illustrate the power of continuing to think: Let's say a pessimist has made up his mind to clean his garage on a Saturday morning. He wakes up and walks out to the garage and opens the door and is shocked to see just how much of a mess it is. "Forget this!" the pessimist says with disgust. "No one could clean this garage in one day!"

And at that point the pessimist slams the garage door shut and goes back inside to do something else. Pessimists are "all-or-nothing" thinkers. They think in catastrophic absolutes. They are either going to do something perfectly or not at all.

Now let's look at how the optimist would face the same problem. He wakes up on the same morning and goes to the same garage and sees the same mess and even utters the same first words to himself, "Forget this! No one could clean this garage in one day!"

But this is where the key difference between an optimist and a pessimist shows itself. Instead of going back into the house, the optimist *keeps thinking.*

"Okay, so I can't clean the whole garage," he says. "What *could* I do that would make a difference?"

He looks for awhile, and thinks things over. Finally it occurs to him that he could break the garage down into four sections and do just one section today.

"For sure I'll do one today," he says, "and even if I only do one section each Saturday, I'll have the whole garage in great shape before the month is over."

A month later, you see a pessimist with a filthy garage and an optimist with a clean garage.

There was a woman in one of my seminars in Las Vegas who told me that this one concept—the optimist's habit of looking for partial solutions—had made an interesting difference in her life.

"I used to come home from work and look at my kitchen and just throw up my hands and curse at it and do nothing at all," she told me. "I'd think the exact same thing as the pessimist in your garage story. Then I decided to just pick a small part of the kitchen and do that, and that area only. It might be a certain counter, or just the sink. By doing just one small part each night

I never resent the work, it's never overwhelming, and my kitchen always looks decent."

Pessimists like to set their problems aside. They think so negatively about "doing the whole thing perfectly" that they end up doing nothing at all!

The optimist always does a little something. She or he always takes an action and always feels like progress is being made.

Because pessimists have a habit of thinking "it's hopeless" or "nothing can be done," they quit thinking too soon. An optimist may have the same initial negative feelings about a project, but he or she keeps thinking until smaller possibilities open up. This is why Alan Loy McGinnis, in his inspiring book *The Power of Optimism,* refers to optimists as "tough-minded."

The pessimist, as far as the use of the human mind goes, is a quitter.

Recent studies show, says McGinnis, that optimists "excel in school, have better health, make more money, establish long and happy marriages, stay connected to their children and perhaps even live longer."

To witness one of the most profound illustrations of the practical effectiveness of optimism in American history, you'll want to rent the movie, *Apollo 13.* Although the job of bringing those astronauts back from the far side of the moon looked daunting and overwhelming, the job was accomplished one small task at a time. The people at Mission Control in Houston who saved the astronauts' lives did so because even in the face of "impossible" technological breakdowns, they kept on thinking. They never gave up. They looked for partial solutions, and they declared that they would string these partial solutions together one at a time until they brought the men home safely.

While the astronauts' lives were still in doubt, there was one glaring pessimist in Houston ground control who made the comment that he feared that Apollo 13 might become the "worst space disaster" in American history. The ground commander in Houston turned to him and said with optimism and anger, "On the contrary, sir, I see Apollo 13 as being our finest hour." And he turned out to be right, which illustrates the life-or-death *effectiveness* of optimistic thinking.

Whenever you feel pessimistic or overwhelmed, remember to *keep thinking.* The more you think about a situation, the more you will see small opportunities for action—and the more small actions you take, the more optimistic energy you will receive. An optimist keeps thinking and self-motivates. A pessimist quits thinking—and then just quits.

In the Broadway musical *South Pacific,* the heroine sings apologetically about being a "cock-eyed optimist." She admits she's "immature and incurably green." This was an early version of a blonde joke. She confesses, as the giddy song soars melodically, that she's "stuck like a dope on a thing called hope and I can't get it out of my heart...not this heart."

That's how our society has viewed optimists—they are dopes. Society thinks optimistic thinking is something that comes from the heart, not the head.

Pessimists, on the other hand, are "realistic." In fact, pessimists will never tell you they are pessimists. In their own minds, they are realists. And when they run into habitual optimists they sneer at them for always "blue-skying" everything, and not facing grim reality.

Pessimists continually use their imaginations to visualize worst-case scenarios, and then concluding that those scenarios are lost causes, they take no action. That's why pessimism always leads to passivity.

But even lying on his couch, bloated with junk food and foggy from too much television, the pessimist knows somewhere in his heart that his "what's the use?" attitude is not effective. He is living a life that is reflected in what Nietzsche once said: "Everything in the world displeased me; but what displeased me most was my displeasure with everything."

Optimists have chosen to make a different use of the human imagination. They agree with Colin Wilson's point of view that "imagination should be used, not to escape from reality, but to create it."

54. Put on a good debate

Negative thinking is something we all do. The difference between the person who is primarily optimistic and the person who is primarily pessimistic is that the optimist learns to become a good debater. Once you become thoroughly aware of the effectiveness of optimism in your life, you can learn to debate your pessimistic thoughts.

The most thorough and useful study I've ever seen on how to do this is contained in Dr. Martin Seligman's classical work, *Learned Optimism*. The studies done by Seligman demonstrate two very profound revelations: 1) optimism is more effective than pessimism; and 2) optimism can be learned.

Seligman based his findings on years of statistical research. He studied professional and amateur athletes, insurance salespeople, and even politicians running for office. His scientific studies proved that optimists dramatically outperform pessimists. So what Norman Vincent Peale had been saying for years in his books on the power of positive thinking was finally proven to be scientifically true.

Peale had based his books on testimonials and supportive biblical passages. The problem with that was that the people he needed to reach the most—skeptics and pessimists—were precisely the kinds of people who would not be anxious to take anything on faith. But once you've digested the remarkable writings of Seligman, you can go back and read Peale with a new sense of excitement. If you don't accept his religious references, it doesn't matter—the personal testimonials are stimulating enough to give his writing great power. Although his most famous book is *The Power of Positive Thinking,* I have derived much more motivation from *Stay Alive All Your Life* and *The Amazing Results of Positive Thinking.*

If you are now skeptical about your power to debate your own pessimistic thoughts, keep in mind that most of us are already great debaters. If somebody comes in and takes one side of an argument, we can usually take the other side and make a case, no matter which side the first person took. Debate teams have to learn to do this. Team members never know until the last second which side of the argument they will be debating, so they learn to be prepared to passionately argue either side.

If you catch yourself brooding, worrying, and thinking pessimistically about an issue, the first step is to recognize your thoughts as being pessimistic. Not wrong or untrue—just pessimistic. And if you are going to get the most out of your *bio-computer* (the brain), you must acknowledge that pessimistic thoughts are less effective.

Once you've accepted the pessimistic nature of your thinking, you are ready to take the next step. (This first step is crucial though. As Nathaniel Branden teaches,

"You can't leave a place you've never been.") The second step is to build a case for the optimistic view.

Start to argue against your first line of reasoning. Pretend you're an attorney whose job is to prove the pessimist in you wrong. Start off on building your case for what's possible. You'll surprise yourself. Optimism is by nature expansive—it opens door after door to what's possible. Pessimism is just the opposite—it is constrictive. It shuts the door on possibility. If you really want to open up your life and motivate yourself to succeed, become an optimistic thinker.

55. Make trouble work for you

One evening, many years ago, my then-14-year-old daughter Stephanie went for a walk with a friend, promising me she would be back home before 10 p.m. I didn't pay much attention to the clock until the 10 o'clock news ended and I realized that she hadn't come home yet. I started to get nervous and irritated. I began pacing the house, wondering what to do. At 11:30 I got in my car and started cruising the neighborhood looking for her. My thoughts were understandably anxious, part fear and part anger. Finally, at 11:45, I drove back past my own house and saw her silhouette in the window. She was home and safe.

But I kept driving. I realized that I was thinking completely pessimistically about the entire incident and I needed to keep thinking before I talked to her. As I drove along I observed all the pessimism I was wallowing in: "She doesn't respect me. She can't keep a promise. My rules and requests mean nothing. This is the tip of the iceberg. I'm going to have problems with her for the next four years at least. Who knows where she went and what she was doing? Were drugs involved? Sex?

Crime? I'm losing sleep over this. This is ruining my peace of mind and my life. Et cetera."

By recognizing how pessimistic my thoughts were, I was able to let the thoughts play completely out before taking a deep breath and telling myself, "Okay. That's one side of the argument. Now it's time to explore the other side." One of my favorite tricks for flipping my mind over to the optimistic side is to ask myself the question: "How can I use this?"

How could I use this incident to improve my relationship with my daughter? How could I make my rules and requests more meaningful to us both? I began to build my case for optimism. I realized that great relationships are built by incidents like these. They are not built by theoretical conversations—but by difficult experiences and what we learn and gain from them.

So I decided to drive a little while longer and let her wait inside. I was sure that by now her sister had told her that I was out looking for her, so she was now the one pacing and anxious. Let her sweat a little, I thought, while I continue to think things through.

I continued to reflect upon my past relationship with Stephanie. One of the great aspects of it was Stephanie's honesty. She had always radiated a quiet and confident kind of serenity about life, and found it easy to be honest with her own feelings and honest with other people. Whenever there had been incidents with other children, teachers, or other parents involved in some misunderstanding, I could always count on Stephanie to tell me the truth. Asking her about what happened always saved me a lot of time.

As I drove the dark neighborhood I also ran through my happiest memories of Stephanie as a little girl, how much I loved her and how proud I was of her when I went to her concerts or talked to her teachers. I recalled the time in grade school when I embarrassed her by asking her principal if he would consider re-naming the school after her. (She had just won an academic award of some kind and I was intoxicated with pride.)

Finally my mind was completely won over to the optimistic side. "How can I use this?" gave me the idea that this incident could be made into something bigger than it seemed—a new commitment to each other to keep agreements and trust each other.

When I finally got home I could see that she was scared. She tried to blame the incident on her not having a watch. She wanted me to appreciate that, somehow, she was a victim of the whole incident. I listened patiently and then I told her I thought it was a much bigger deal than that. I talked about my relationship with her and how I had cherished her truthfulness throughout her childhood. I told her that I thought we might have lost all of that tonight. That we might have to figure a way to start over.

"It's not that big a deal," she protested. But I told her that I thought it was a very big deal, because it was all about our relationship and whether we were going to keep agreements with each other.

I told Stephanie I wanted her to be as happy as she could possibly be, and the only way I could really help that happen would be if we kept agreements with each other. I told her how scared I was, how angry I was, how her staying out had ruled out a good night's sleep for me. I asked her to try to understand. I talked about our life together when she was a little girl, and I reminded her how extraordinarily truthful she was. I mentioned a few incidents when she got in trouble but how I had gone right to her for the truth and always got it.

We talked for a long time that night, and she finally saw that coming home when she says she's coming home—indeed, doing what she says she's going to do— is a really "big deal." It's everything.

Since that incident and conversation, Stephanie has been extremely sensitive to keeping her word. If she goes out and promises to be back at a certain time, she takes along a watch or makes certain someone she's with has one. The "incident" that night is something neither of us will forget, because it got us clear on the idea of trust and agreements. You could even say that it was a *good* thing.

We have heard of so many incidents where bad events in retrospect were strokes of great fortune. A person who broke her leg skiing met a doctor in the hospital, fell in love, married him, and had a happy relationship for life. Because most of us have experienced a number of these incidents, we're aware of the dynamic. What seems bad (like a broken leg) turns out unexpectedly great. We begin to see the truth that every problem carries a gift inside it.

By choosing to *make use of* seemingly bad events, you can access that gift much sooner. By asking yourself "How can I use this?" or "What might be good about this?" you can turn your life around on a dime.

56. Storm your own brain

The term "brainstorming" is now very well known in American business life.

I first learned it many years ago when I worked as a copywriter in an ad agency. Whenever we would get a new account our agency's president would get us all together to "brainstorm" for creative ideas for the client.

The main rules of the brainstorming session are 1) there are no stupid ideas—the more unreasonable the better—and 2) everyone must play.

I have sometimes facilitated brainstorming sessions with business managers. We go around the table and each person puts out an idea and the facilitator writes it on the flip pad. We go around and around until all the reasonable ideas are exhausted and the unreasonable ideas start to flow. It is usually among the unreasonable ideas that something great is discovered. Brainstorming works so well because the usual restraints against stupidity are lifted. It's okay to be unreasonable and far out.

What most people in business don't realize is that this powerful technique can be used by an individual, alone with himself or herself. I first discovered this while driving in my car a number of years ago listening to a motivational tape by Earl Nightingale. He talked about a system he had learned that worked wonders.

On the top of a piece of paper you put a problem you want solved or a goal you want reached. You then put numbers 1 through 20 on the paper and begin your brainstorming session. The rules are the same as with a group session. You have to list 20 ideas, and they don't have to be well thought out or even reasonable. Give yourself permission to flow. Your only objective is to have 20 ideas scrawled down within a certain short amount of time.

If you do this for a week, you will end up with 100 ideas! Are all of them usable? Of course not, but who cares? When you began the process you probably didn't have *any* usable ideas.

I have used this system myself over and over with really great results. It works so well because it relaxes the normal tensions against creative, outrageous thinking. It invites the right side of your brain to play along.

Recently a friend called for some advice about his career. He was in show business and had developed his act to the point where he was one of the top performers in the nation. His problem was marketing and self-promotion. That part of his career was lagging behind his talent.

"What if I told you that there is someone who can give you 100 specific marketing ideas tailored to your precise career and audience?" I asked him. He was very interested.

"You, yourself are that person," I said.

I then told him about the list-of-20 self-storming technique I had personally been using for a number of years. He eagerly jotted down the rules of the game and got busy playing.

Two weeks later he called me very excited about the results. "I've got some really great marketing ideas right now, more than I've ever had in the past," he said. "Thanks."

Self-mentoring is the best mentoring you can get because your mentor knows you so well. And although it's often beneficial to get specific outside personal coaching, the best coaching teaches us to look within. A great mentor once said, "The kingdom of heaven is within you."

57. Keep changing your voice

There have been times when I have been told that I am lucky to have a good speaking voice. And some people are impressed that I rarely use a microphone in my seminars, even with hundreds of people in the audience.

People will conclude that I have been "blessed" with a powerful set of vocal cords. But it is not true. As I related in an earlier chapter, my voice used to be no better than a feeble monotone. That is, until I got motivated to change it. There were two instances that inspired my system for developing my voice. The first was a magazine interview I read many years ago about the actor Richard Burton (who had perhaps the most mesmerizing speaking voice of all time—listen to the Broadway recording of "Camelot" and hear him as King Arthur speak and "sing" his songs.) In the interview, Burton said that his voice was how he made his living, so he made certain that each morning while showering he sang a number of songs to keep his vocal cords strong and supple. Later, on a television talk show, actor Tony Randall told the host how he developed his trademark sing-song acting voice: "I took up opera," he said. "I found that singing opera did more for my stage voice than anything else I ever tried."

Those two interviews have stayed in my mind ever since, and I always carry a number of tapes and CDs in my car to sing along with. I crank them up good and loud (this is best done while driving alone) and sing at the top of my lungs. I make certain that I do this every day, even when I don't feel like singing. In the words of William James, there's another benefit: "We don't sing because we're happy, we're happy because we sing."

Prior to a major public speech, I'll often get to my location more than an hour ahead of time and then just drive around the neighborhood singing like a madman. (Sometimes I worry that my host client might drive by and spot me in my car singing along with Elvis and looking dangerously psychotic. But the benefits are worth that risk.) I find that when I drive and sing like that my breathing is better, my timing is better, and when I speak, my voice effortlessly fills the hall.

You might think, "I don't speak for a living." So such a weird practice might not be necessary for you. But we all speak. A pleasant, relaxed, and strong speaking voice is a priceless asset to anyone whose job involves communicating with other humans.

When referring to people whose speaking voices are pleasing to listen to, many people use words like "melodious" and "well-modulated." This is a good hint to tell if someone is complimenting a great speaking voice.

You are not stuck with the voice you have now. Start singing, and soon you'll be creating the voice you'd like to have. The stronger your voice, the stronger your confidence and the stronger your confidence, the easier it is to motivate yourself.

58. Embrace the new frontier

Fortunately, for all of us, a new frontier is upon us. Because our nation, and world, has entered the information age, the old patterns for living are gone.

An article by business writer John Huey appeared in the June 27, 1994 edition of *Fortune*. In it, Huey observed, "Let's say you're going to a party, so you pull out some pocket change and buy a little greeting card that plays 'Happy Birthday' when it's opened. After the party, someone casually tosses the card into the trash, throwing away more computer power than existed in the entire world before 1950."

In the old paradigm, forged in the Industrial Age, we human beings became less and less useful and adventurous. We found lifelong employment in guaranteed jobs and did our jobs the same way until retirement. Then, once we reached retirement age, we became thoroughly useless to society and lived lives dependent on the government, our relatives, or our own savings that we accumulated in our "useful" years.

Now, with the technological explosion and entry into the Information Age, employers are no longer as interested in our job histories as they used to be. They are now more interested in our current capabilities.

One of the romantic appeals of the early Daniel Boone and Davy Crockett frontier days in our nation was the usefulness of individuals. If you were living out on the frontier, farming, cooking, and hunting, and you turned 65, it would never occur to anyone to ask you to "retire."

We have finally come back to those days of honoring usefulness over age and status. For example, if my company is trying to enter the Chinese market to sell its software and you, at age 70, can speak fluent Chinese, know all about software, and have energy and a zest for success, how can I afford to ignore you?

Bill Gates of Microsoft has said, "Our company has only one asset—human imagination." If you took all of Microsoft's buildings, real estate, office hardware, physical assets—anything you can *touch*—away from the company, where would it be? Almost exactly where it is now. Because in today's world a company's value is in it's thinking, not in its possessions.

This is great news for the individual—because usefulness is back in style. If you can cultivate your skills, keep learning new things, study computers, learn a foreign language, or become expert in a foreign culture and market—*you can make yourself useful.*

The great basketball coach John Wooden recommended that we live by this credo—especially apt for the new technological frontier: "Learn as if you were to live forever. Live as if you were to die tomorrow."

Gone are the days when your employability depended primarily on your job history, your school ties, your connections, your family, or your seniority. Today your employability depends on one thing—your current skills. And those skills are completely under your control.

This is the new frontier. And where we once entered retirement age nervous about the "wolves at our door," today, with a commitment to lifelong growth through learning, we can be as useful to the world community as we are motivated to be.

The more we learn about the future, the more motivated we become to be a valuable part of it.

59. Upgrade your old habits

Super motivation is much more difficult to achieve when we are held back mentally by bad habits. Trying to move toward the life we want while dragging along our bad habits was described in the Scottish rock group Del Amitri's song lyrics, "It's like driving with the brakes on, it's like swimming with your boots on..."

But here's the catch: Bad habits simply cannot be broken. Nor can they be gotten rid of. Ask the millions who continue to try. They always end up, in the words of Richard Brautigan, "trying to shovel mercury with a pitchfork," because our bad habits exist for good reasons. They're there to do something for us, even if that something ends up being self-destructive. Down deep, even a bad habit is trying to make us operate better.

People who smoke are trying, even through their addiction, to do something beneficial—perhaps to breathe deeply and relax. Such breathing is needed to balance stress, so their smoking is a way in which they are trying to make themselves better. Bad habits are like that—they are based on a perceived benefit. That's why they're so hard to just "get rid of."

That's why habits must be respected and understood before they can be transformed. What created the habit must be built upon, not killed. We must go to the beneficial impulse that drives the habit, and then expand on that to make the habit grow from something bad into something good.

Let's take drinking as an example. I've known people who used to be drunk all the time who are now sober all the time. How did they do it? Couldn't we just say that they just got rid of their drinking habit? Not really. Because, without exception, the recovered people I know *replaced* their drinking with something else.

Taking all of one's courage, relaxation, and spirituality from a bottle of alcohol is a very damaging habit. But to simply eliminate it leads to even worse problems: shakes, DTs, fear, dread, paranoia. A total void.

People who join Alcoholics Anonymous, however, replace their "false courage"—once found in a bottle of alcohol—with *real* courage found in the meeting rooms of AA. The completely artificial sense of spirituality formerly found in a tumbler of spirits is replaced by the true and deeply personal spirituality found in working the 12-step program of enlightenment. The superficial but highly emotional relationships the alcoholic had made in his favorite bars are replaced by real friendships.

Replacement is powerful because it works, and where bad habits are concerned it's the *only* thing that works. I've known people who quit smoking without intending to. They took up running, or some form of regular aerobic exercise, and soon the breathing and relaxation they were getting from the exercise made the smoking feel bad to their bodies. They quit smoking be-cause they had introduced a replacement.

People who diet have the same experience. It isn't staying away from fattening food that works—it's in-troducing a regular diet of delicious, healthy food that works. It's replacement.

Subconsciously you don't think your bad habits are bad! And that's because they're filling a perceived need. So the way to strengthen yourself is to identify the need and honor it. Honor the need by *replacing* the current habit with one that is healthier and more effective. Re-place one habit, and soon you'll be motivated to replace another.

60. Paint your masterpiece today

Think of your day as a blank artist's canvas.

If you go through your day passively accepting what-ever other people and circumstances splatter on your canvas, you will more than likely see a mess where art could be.

If the mess troubles your sleep, your next new day will begin in a state of fatigue and mild confusion. From such a state, your canvas will be splattered all the more with shapes you don't like and colors you never chose.

Thinking of your day as a painter's canvas will allow you to be more conscious of what is happening to you when you flood your mind with nothing but Internet gossip, commercials on the radio, the latest murder trial, your spouse's criticisms, office politics, and pessi-mistic musical lyrics.

If you'll allow yourself to step back far enough to realize and truly see that your daily canvas is filling up with all these negative things, a certain freedom occurs. It's the freedom to choose something better.

The more *conscious* we are of our freedom to paint whatever we want on our canvas, the less we go through life as a victim of circumstances. Many of us aren't even aware of our own victim status. We read whatever's on the coffee table, listen to whatever's on the car radio, eat whatever's handy, scan whatever's on the Internet, talk to whomever calls us on the phone, and watch whatever's on the television—often too passive to even click the remote control.

We must be aware that we have it in us to change all that. We can paint our day our way. The best time management—or "day-painting"—course I ever took was taught by Dennis Deaton. His seminar's main point is that we can't manage time—we can only manage ourselves.

"Clear the clutter from your mind," Deaton says, "and remove the obstacles to greater success."

While most time management courses feel like courses in engineering, Deaton has captured the spirit of the artist in his teaching. His prescriptions for managing your day all stem from goal-creation and living the visions you create.

Wake up and visualize your day as a blank canvas. Ask yourself, "Who's the artist today? Blind circumstance, or me? If I choose to be the artist, how do I want to paint my day?"

61. Swim laps underwater

When Bobby Fisher prepared for his world championship chess match with Boris Spassky, he prepared by swimming laps underwater every day.

He knew that as the chess matches wore on into the late hours, the player with the most oxygen going to his brain would have the mental advantage. So he built his chess game by building his lungs.

When he defeated Spassky, many were surprised by his astonishing wit and mental staying power, especially late in the matches when both players should've been weary and burned out. What kept Bobby Fisher alert wasn't caffeine or amphetamines—it was his breathing.

General George Patton once gave a lecture to his troops on brainpower. He, too, knew the connection between breathing and thinking.

"In war, as in peace, a man needs all the brains he can get," said Patton. "Nobody ever had too many brains. Brains come from oxygen. Oxygen comes from the lungs where the air goes when we breathe. The oxygen in the air gets into the blood and travels to the brain. Any fool can double the size of his lungs."

I learned about Patton's passion for teaching his troops deep breathing from Porter Williamson. I had once written a few political radio and television commercials that caught Mr. Williamson's attention, so he called me and asked me to lunch one day. Because he had identified himself as the author of *Patton's Principles*, I eagerly accepted his invitation, having coincidentally read the marvelous book a few weeks earlier. Williamson had served in the army for many years as Patton's most trusted legal adviser.

Williamson told me many stories about serving with Patton, and how truly extraordinary a motivator the general was. Most of the Patton quotes in this book come from Williamson's own memories of his service with the great general. Williamson told me about how he himself had lost his leg to bone cancer, and how the doctors had erroneously forecasted his death twice. His inner strength, he said, often came from the inspiration he received in his days of serving with Patton.

"Frequently, General Patton would stop at my desk," recalled Williamson, "and ask, 'How long you been sitting at that desk? Get up and get out of here! Your brain stops working after you sit in a swivel chair for 20 minutes. Keep the body moving around so the juices will run to the right places. It'll be good for the brain! If you sit in that chair too long all of your brainpower will be in your shoes. You cannot keep your mind active when your body is inactive.' "

That one principle—an active mind cannot exist in an inactive body—became Bobby Fisher's secret weapon in winning the world championship of chess. Who would have guessed that swimming underwater would make you a better chess player? Certainly not the overweight, worn-out chess "genius" Boris Spassky.

Sometimes, all you need is the air that you breathe to motivate yourself. Going for a run or a walk or simply deep breathing gives the brain the fuel it feeds on to be newly refreshed and creative.

62. Bring on a good coach

After a rare disappointing round on the golf course, Tiger Woods will often take a golf lesson.

When I first heard about this, I asked myself, who could give Tiger Woods a lesson in golf?

But that was before I ever really understood the value of coaching. The person who taught me that value was a young business consultant named Steve Hardison. Hardison taught me this: Tiger takes a lesson not because his coach is a better player who can give advice and tips, but because his coach *can stand back from Tiger Woods and see him objectively.*

Steve Hardison had created an art form of coming into corporations and seeing things objectively. In fact, his perception ran deeper than that. He had near-psychic power to "see what was missing." It was a gift he could also apply to individuals, but only if they were ready for the rigors of his coaching.

I used to teasingly call one of his illustrative personal stories "The Parable of the Mission." As a young missionary for his church in England, Hardison broke all records for enrolling congregants. He contrasted his own method with that of the other missionaries.

While the others would rush out and knock on doors all day, Hardison would spend the first part of each day planning and plotting his activities. By *creating* his day before it happened, he was able to combine visits, economize on travel time, and increase the number of enrollment conversations in a given day. He also used his creative planning time to set up intra-neighborhood referrals for himself so that many of his visits came with a reference.

The other missionaries were very active, but they were focused on the activity, not the result. They were in the business of knocking on doors and scurrying about—Steve was in the business of enrolling people into the church. The records he set for enrollment were no accident. He planned things that way.

Steve helped me understand something that lives inside of all of us, something he called "the voice." When you wake up in the morning, the voice is there right away, telling you that you are too tired to get up or too sick to go to work. During a sales meeting when you are just about to say something bold to a client, the voice might tell you to cool it. "Hold back." "Be careful."

"The trick is," said Steve, "to not ignore or deny the existence of the voice. Because it's there, in all of us. No one is free of the voice. However, you don't have to obey the voice. You can talk back to the voice. And when you really get good, you can even talk trash to the voice.

Make fun of it. Ridicule it. Point out how stupid it is. And once you get into that way of debating your own doubts, you start to take back control of your life."

Many times I'd be in the middle of a large business project and ask to meet with Steve for an hour. After he listened for a few minutes, he would almost invariably see right away what was "missing" in my behavior. Like a great golf teacher watching Tiger Woods' backswing, he would say, "Are you willing to accept some coaching on this?" And I would eagerly say yes. Then he would tell me truthfully, sometimes ruthlessly, what he saw. I didn't always like what he saw, but I always grew stronger from talking about it.

Hardison's coaching was so jolting that sometimes it reminded me of an incident that happened to me when I was a boy playing Little League baseball.

I had injured my knee in a play at third base and when the game was over the knee was swollen and my entire leg was stiff. As I sat on the bench with my leg straight out in front of me, a doctor whose son was on our team was kneeling down by my leg as my father looked on.

"I'd like you to bend your leg now," he said to me as his hands gently held my swollen knee.

"I can't," I told him.

"You can't?" he asked, looking up at me. "Why can't you?"

"Because I tried, and it really hurts."

The doctor looked at me for a second, and then said simply but gently, "Then hurt yourself."

I was startled by his request. Hurt myself? On purpose? But then, without saying anything, I slowly bent my leg. Yes, there was tremendous pain, but that didn't matter. I was still mesmerized by his request.

The doctor massaged my knee with his fingers and nodded to my father that everything would be okay. I'd have to have x-rays and the usual precautionary exam, but he saw nothing seriously wrong for now.

But I was still aware that something very big had just happened to me. After a boyhood that was characterized by avoiding pain and discomfort of any kind, all of a sudden I saw that I could hurt myself if I needed to, and that I could do it calmly without batting an eye. Perhaps I wasn't the coward I'd always thought I was. Perhaps there was as much courage in me as in anyone else, and it was all a matter of being willing to call on it.

It was a defining incident in my life, and it was not dissimilar to the way Steve Hardison, as a coach, has required that I call on things inside me that I didn't know I had.

One time I was having a hard time enrolling people into seminars and doing my prospecting calls on the phone. Steve grabbed the phone and started calling people and signing them up. Then he accidentally dialed a wrong number and reached some mechanic at a car repair garage. Most people would have apologized at that point and hung up and dialed again. But rather than waste the call, Steve introduced himself and then stayed on the phone—*until the mechanic had signed up for a seminar.*

Hardison is a gifted and courageous public speaker, a resourceful and relentless salesperson, a talented athlete and a committed family man and church member. The kind of guy who used to make me sick!

I could write an entire book about Steve Hardison's remarkable work in coaching and consulting, and someday I just might. Examples of ways that he coached me to higher levels of performance are plentiful. But I think the greatest thing he has taught me is the value of coaching itself.

Once you open yourself up to being coached, you begin to receive the same advantages enjoyed by great actors and athletes everywhere. When you open yourself up to coaching, you don't become weaker—you grow stronger. You become more responsible for changing yourself.

In *The Road Less Traveled*, M. Scott Peck writes, "The problem of distinguishing what we are and what we are not responsible for in this life is one of the greatest problems of human existence...we must possess the willingness and the capacity to suffer continual self-examination."

The best coaches show us how to examine ourselves. It takes courage to ask for coaching, but the rewards can be great. The best moments come when your coach helps you do something you have previously been afraid to do. When Hardison would recommend that I do something I was afraid to do I'd say, "I don't know if I could do that."

"So don't be *you*," he would say. "If you can't do that, then be someone else. Be someone who could do it. Be DeNiro, be Bruce Lee, be anybody, I don't care, as long as you do it."

Coaching's contribution to my life is illustrated in these words by French philosopher Guillaume Apollinaire:

" 'Come to the edge,' he said.

They said, 'We are afraid.'

'Come to the edge,' he said.

They came.

He pushed them.

And they flew."

You can get coaching anytime. If coaching is appropriate for your golf or tennis game, it is even more appropriate for the game of life. Ask someone to be honest with you and coach you for a while. Let them check your "swing." Let them tell you what they see. It's a courageous thing to do, and it will always lead to more self-motivation and growth.

63. Try to sell your home

Once when Steve Hardison and I were discussing a few of my old habits that were holding me back from realizing my business goals, I blurted out to him, "But why do I *do* those things? If I know they hold me back, why do I continue to do them?"

"Because they are *home* to you," he said. "They feel like home. When you do those things, you do them because that's what you're comfortable doing, and so you make yourself right at home doing them. And as they say, there's no place like home."

"Home" can be an ugly place if it's not kept up and consciously made beautiful. "Home" can be a dark, damp prison, smelling of bad habits and laziness. But we *still* don't want to leave it, no matter how bad it gets, because we think we are safe there.

However, when we inspect the worn-out house more closely, we can see that the safety we think we're experiencing is pure self-limitation.

It's very hard to leave home—many of us try and fail many times. Noel Paul Stookey wrote a hauntingly beautiful song called "The House Song," which captures this feeling. The opening words are, "This house goes on sale every Wednesday morning...and is taken off the market in the afternoon."

After grasping Hardison's metaphor of home, I immediately saw that I needed to move out of *my* house. I needed to move up in the neighborhood. I needed a better home. A home that contained habits that would keep me focused on goal-oriented activity. Hardison helped coach me in that direction until the new activities began to feel like where I should have been living all along.

Hardison's metaphor of "home" as the equivalent of old disempowering habits has stayed with me for a long time. Recently while I was putting together a tape of motivational music to play in my car, I included the energetic "I'm Going Home" by Alvin Lee and Ten Years After. As I drove around listening to it turned up all the way, I thought about what Hardison taught. I let the song be about the new home I would always be in the process of moving to.

Don't be afraid to leave the psychic home you're in. Get excited about building a larger, newer, happier home in your mind, and then go live there.

In Colin Wilson's brilliant but little-known, out-of-print novel *Necessary Doubt,* he created Gustav Neumann, a fascinating character who made many discoveries about human beings. At one point Neumann says, "I came to realize that people build themselves personalities as they build houses—to protect themselves from the world. They become its prisoners. And most people are in such a hurry to hide inside their four walls that they build the house too quickly."

Identify the habits that keep you trapped. Identify what you have decided is your final personality and accept that it might be a hasty construction built only to keep you safe from risk and growth. Once you've done that, you can leave. You can get the blueprints out and create the home you really want.

64. Get your soul to talk

We've always been a little nervous, culturally, about talking to ourselves. We usually associate it with insanity. But it was Plato who said that his definition of *thinking* was "the soul talking to itself."

If you really want to get your life worked out, there is no one better to talk to than yourself. No other person has as much information about your problems and no other person knows your skills and capabilities better. And there's no one else who can *do* more for you than yourself.

A lot of people in the motivational and psychological professions recommend affirmations. You choose a sentence to say, such as, "Every day in every way I'm getting better and better," and repeat it whether or not you think it's true. While affirmations are a good first step to re-programming, I prefer conversations. Conversations work faster.

The two most inspirational guidelines to productive self-conversational exercises are in Martin Seligman's *Learned Optimism* and Nathaniel Branden's *The Six Pillars of Self-Esteem.* Seligman offers ways to dispute your own pessimism and create the habit of optimistic thinking. Branden offers provocative sentence stems for you to complete.

Rather than brainlessly parroting "I'm getting better and better" to myself, it makes a longer-lasting impression when I logically argue the case and win. With enough back-and-forth conversation, I can *prove* to myself that I am getting better. Proof beats the parrot every time. It's one thing to try to hypnotize myself through repetition of words to accept something as true, and it's quite another to *convince* myself that it is true.

Branden suggests that we get our creative thinking going each morning by asking ourselves two questions: 1) What's good in my life? and 2) What is there still to be done?

Most people don't talk to themselves at all. They listen to the radio, watch TV, gossip, and fill up on the words and thoughts of *other people* all day long. But it's impossible to indulge in that kind of activity and also get motivated. Motivation is something you talk yourself into.

65. Promise the moon

One frightening and effective way to motivate yourself is to make an unreasonable promise—to go to someone you care about, either personally or professionally, and promise them something really big, something that will take all the effort and creativity you've got to make happen.

When President John Kennedy promised that America would put a man on the moon, the power of that thrilling promise alone energized all of NASA for the entire time it took to accomplish the amazing feat. In his book about the Apollo 13 mission, *Lost Moon*, astronaut Jim Lovell called Kennedy's original promise "outrageous." But it showed how effective being outrageous could be.

In his book *Passion, Profit, and Power,* Marshall Sylver recalls seeing a billboard in Las Vegas put up by one of the casino owners who wanted to become a nonsmoker. The billboard read: "If You See Me Smoking in the Next 90 Days, I'll Pay You $100,000!" Can you see the power in that promise?

A couple of years ago I promised my children that I would send them to camp in Michigan. They had been to the camp near Traverse City before, and loved it. When you live during the year in Arizona, there's something magical about the water and emerald forests of northern Michigan. It was an expensive camp, but when I made the promise I was doing well financially, and I was confident that they could all go.

Then as the summer neared I'd run short of money and had to rearrange my priorities. My speaking schedule had replaced much of the commissioned selling I was doing and it looked like camp might not be in the picture.

I remember specifically talking to my boy Bobby, who was 8 years old at the time, about how times were temporarily hard and how camp didn't look like a good possibility any more this year. He was in the front seat of the car and I'll never forget for as long as I live the look on his face. He said very softly, so softly that I could barely hear him, "but you promised."

He was right. I didn't say I'd try, I didn't say it was a goal, I promised. And the feelings I had at that moment were so overwhelming that I finally said to him, "Yes, I did promise. And because you reminded me that it was a promise, I will say to you right now that you're going to camp. I'll do what it takes. I'm sorry that I forgot it was a promise."

The first thing I did was change jobs, and my first condition on accepting my new job was that my bonus for signing was the exact amount of money it took to send my children to camp. It was done.

66. Make somebody's day

To basketball coach John Wooden, making each day your masterpiece was not just about selfish personal achievement. In his autobiography, *They Call Me Coach*, he mentions an element vital to creating each day.

"You cannot live a perfect day," he said, "without doing something for someone who will never be able to repay you."

I agree with that. But there's a way to *make sure* you can't be repaid—and that's doing something for someone who won't even know who did it.

This gets into a theory I've had all my life, that you can create luck in your life. Not from the idea that luck is needed for success, because it isn't. But from the idea that luck can be a welcome addition to your life.

You can create luck for yourself by creating it for someone else. If you know about someone who is hurting financially, and you arrange for a few hundred dollars to arrive at their home, and they don't even know who you are, then you've made them lucky. By making someone lucky, something will then happen in your own life that also feels like pure luck. (I can't explain why this happens, and I have no scientific basis for it, so all I can say is try it a few times and see if you aren't as startled as I have been at the results...it doesn't have to be money, either. We have a lot of other things to give, always.)

When *you* get lucky, you'll get more motivated, because you feel like the universe is more on your side. Experiment with this a little. Don't be imprisoned by cynicism posing as rationality on this subject. See what happens to you when you make other people get lucky.

67. Play the circle game

If you use my four-minute, four-circle, goal-setting system described earlier you can be the creator of your universe.

"You know, that's blasphemous," a seminar student once told me during a break. "Only God can create the universe."

"But if you believe that," I said, "you must also believe as it is written, that we were all created in God's image. And if you believe in God as the Creator, and that He created us in His image, then what are we doing when we don't create? Whose image are we living in when we deliberately do not create?"

Try this: After you wake up in the morning, wipe the sleep from your eyes, sit down with a pad of paper, and draw four circles. These are your own "planets." Label the first circle, "Lifelong Dream." (And in order to keep this example simple, I'll make it strictly financial, although you can do it with any kinds of goals you want.) Your lifelong dream might be to save a half a million dollars for your retirement years. So, put that number in your "Life" circle. Then look at circle two, the next planet in your solar system. That circle you will label, "My Year." What do you need to save in the next year in order to be on course to hit your life savings goal? (When you factor in the interest, it's less than you think.) And when you arrive at the figure, make certain that it matches up mathematically with your first circle. In other words, if you save this amount, and save, say 10 percent more each year that follows, will you achieve your "Life" number? If not, do some more math until you get a direct connection between your yearly savings projection and your lifelong goal.

Now that you've got your first two circles filled with a number, move to the third circle, "My Month." What would you have to save each month to hit your year's goal? Then put that number down. Three circles are now filled.

Now go to the final circle, "My Day." What do you need to do today—that if you repeated it every day— would ensure a successful month?

(By the way, as I said, this doesn't have to just be about money, it can be about physical fitness, learning a language, relationship networking, spirituality, nutrition, or anything important to you.)

The power of this system lies in thinking of it as a universe, which, as Wayne Dyer keeps reminding us, means "one song." When you work the math, you cannot help but see that each circle, if done successfully, *guarantees* the success of the next circle. If you hit your daily goal every day, your monthly goal is automatically hit— in fact you don't even have to worry about it. And if your monthly goal is reached, the yearly goal has to happen. And if your yearly goals are hit, the lifelong goal cannot *not* be reached.

When you study the irrefutable mathematical truth contained in this system, a strange feeling comes over you. You realize that all four circles are ultimately dependent on the success of just one circle: the circle labeled, "My Day."

Then you get the strangely empowering sensation that you have just proved on paper that your day and your life are the same thing. There is no future other than the future you are working on today. Your future is not stranded out there somewhere in space.

This is what the great poet Rainer Maria Rilke meant when he said, "The future enters into us, in order to transform itself in us, long before it happens."

Remember that once you have worked out the math for this, the circle game is only a four-minute daily exercise. Many times in seminars I give, participants will say that they are too busy for all this goal-setting activity. They have lives to live! But I like to remind them of the words of Henry Ford who said, "If you do not think about the future, you won't have one."

And I also like to stress that I am only talking about four minutes a day.

The purpose of making the circles mathematically sound is that you can remove the elements of "faith" and "hoping" from your action plan. You *know* your goals will be hit. Who would you want to bet on, the tennis player who has faith that she's going to win or the one who *knows* she's going to win?

By drawing these simple four circles you can create your universe anywhere, anytime. Waiting in line at the bank, sitting in the doctor's office, waiting for a meeting to begin, or just doodling. Each time you do it, your universe gets closer to you. Each time you draw the circles you are hit with this revelation: There is absolutely no difference between succeeding today and having a successful life.

In *The Magic of Believing,* Claude Bristol recounts a particularly absent-minded habit of his that, looking back, may have had a bigger impact on shaping his universe than he ever realized. He said that whether he was on the phone, or just sitting in moments of abstraction, he would always have a pen or pencil out doodling.

"My doodling was in the form of dollar signs like these—$$$$$—on every paper that came across my desk. The cardboard covers of all the files that were placed before me daily were covered with these markings; so were the covers of telephone directories, scratch pads, and even the face of important correspondence."

Bristol's later studies on "mind stuff experiments," "the power of suggestion," and "the art of mental pictures" caused him to conclude that his lifelong habit of doodling dollar signs had had an enormous impact on programming his mind to always be opportunistic and enterprising when it came to money. The fortune he acquired demands that we take his observations seriously.

68. Get up a game

It is said that John F. Kennedy's father's credo was, "Don't get mad, get even."

And that credo has a certain vengeful, clever wisdom in it as far as it goes, but you might go even further with this credo: "Don't just get even—get better."

When Michael Jordan was a sophomore in high school he was *cut* from his high school basketball team. Michael Jordan was told by his coach that he wasn't good enough to play high school basketball. It was a crushing disappointment for a young boy whose heart was set on making the team, but he used the incident—not to get mad, not to get even, but to get better.

We all have those moments when people tell us, or insinuate to us, that they don't think we measure up—that they don't believe in us. Some of us have entire childhoods filled with that experience. The most common reaction is anger and resentment. Sometimes it motivates us to "get even" or to prove somebody wrong. But there's a better way to respond, a way that is creative rather than reactive.

"How can I use this?" is the question that puts us on the road to creativity. It transforms the anger into optimistic energy, so we can grow beyond someone else's negative expectations.

Johnny Bench, a Hall of Fame baseball player, knew what it was like to not be believed in.

"In the second grade," he said, "they asked us what we wanted to be. I said I wanted to be a ballplayer and they laughed. In the eighth grade they asked the same question, and I said a ballplayer, and they laughed a little more. By the 11th grade, no one was laughing."

Our country has gone through a difficult period of time since World War II. We no longer value heroes and individual achievement as we once did. "Competition" has become a bad word. But competition, if confronted enthusiastically, can be the greatest self-motivating experience in the world.

What some people fear in the idea of competition, I suppose, is that we will become obsessed with succeeding at somebody else's expense. That we'll take too much pleasure in defeating and therefore "being better" than somebody else. Many times during conversations with my children's teachers, I am told how the school has progressively removed grades and awards from some activities "so that the kids don't feel they have to compare themselves to each other." They are proud of how they've softened their educational programs so that there's less stress and competition. But what they are doing is not softening the program—they are softening the children.

If you are interested in self-motivation, self-creation, and being the best you can be, there is nothing *better* than competition. It teaches you the valuable lesson that no matter how good you are, there is always somebody better than you are. That's the lesson in humility you need, the lesson those teachers are misguidedly trying to teach by removing grades.

It teaches you that by trying to beat somebody else, you reach for more inside of yourself. Trying to beat somebody else simply puts the "game" back into life. If it's done optimistically, it gives energy to both competitors. It teaches sportsmanship. And it gives you a benchmark for measuring your own growth.

The poet William Butler Yeats used to be amused at how many definitions people came up with for happiness. But happiness wasn't any of the things people said it was, insisted Yeats.

"Happiness is just one thing," he said. "Growth. We are happy when we are growing."

A good competitor will cause you to grow. He will stretch you beyond your former skill level. If you want to get good at chess, play against somebody better at chess than you are. In the movie *Searching for Bobby Fisher,* we see the negative effects of resisting competition on a young chess genius until he starts to *use* the competition to grow. Once he stops taking it personally and seriously, the game itself becomes energizing. Once he embraces the intriguing fun of competition, he gets better and better as a player, and grows as a person.

I mentioned earlier that I'd heard a report on the radio that there was a Little League organization somewhere in Pennsylvania that had decided not to keep score in its games anymore because losing might damage the players' self-esteem. They had it all wrong: Losing teaches kids to *grow* in the face of defeat. It also teaches them that losing isn't the same as dying, or being worthless. It's just the other side of winning. If we teach children to fear competition because of the possibility of losing, then we actually *lower* their self-esteem.

Compete wherever you can. But always compete in the spirit of fun, knowing that finally surpassing someone else is far less important than surpassing yourself.

If you're better at a game than I am, when I play against you and try to beat you it's really not you I'm after. Who I'm really beating is *the old me.* Because the old me couldn't beat you.

69. Turn your mother down

Psychologist and author M. Scott Peck observes, "To a child, his or her parents represent the world. He assumes that the way his parents do things is the way things are done."

In Dr. Martin Seligman's studies of optimism and pessimism, he found out the same thing: We learn how to explain the world to ourselves from our parents—and more specifically, our mothers.

"This tells us that young children listen to what their primary caretaker (usually the mother) says about causes," writes Seligman, "and they tend to make this style their own. If the child has an optimistic mother, this is great, but it can be a disaster for the child if the child has a pessimistic mother." Fortunately, Seligman's studies show that the disaster need only be temporary—that optimism can be learned...at any age.

But it is not self-motivating to blame Mom if you find yourself to be a pessimist. What works better is self-creation: to produce a voice in your head that's so confident and strong that your mother's voice gets edited out, and your own voice becomes the only one you hear.

And as much as you want to eliminate the continuing influence of a pessimistic adult from your childhood, remember that blaming someone else never motivates you because it strengthens the belief that your life is being shaped by people outside yourself. Love your mom (she learned her pessimism from *her* mother)—and change yourself.

70. Face the sun

"When you face the sun," wrote Helen Keller, "the shadows always fall behind you."

This was Helen Keller's poetic way of recommending optimistic thinking. What you look at and what you face grows in your life. What you ignore falls behind you. But if you turn and look only at the shadows, they *become* your life.

When I was younger I remember hearing other kids tell a joke about Helen Keller. "Have you heard about the Helen Keller doll?" they would ask. "You wind it up and it bumps into things."

I've often thought about that joke, and why such a joke about someone who was deaf and blind was funny. I think the answer lies in our nervousness about other people overcoming huge misfortunes. (Perhaps we laugh nervously because we haven't overcome our own small ones.)

In our own day and age, we are quick to consider ourselves victims. We are all victims of some sort of emotional, social, gender, or racial abuse. We enjoy taking what difficulties we have had in life and blowing them up into huge injustices.

Helen Keller didn't complain about being from a dysfunctional family, or of being a woman, or of not being given enough money from the government to compensate her for her handicaps. She had challenges most of us can't even imagine, but she refused to become fascinated by them and make her handicaps her life. She didn't want to focus on the shadows when there was so much sun.

There is a bumper sticker that I see every so often as I'm driving around: "Life is a bitch and then you die." I always wonder about that bumper sticker because it seems illogical. If life is that bad, death should be welcome. The sticker should say, "Life is a bitch, *but* the good news is you die."

British author G.K. Chesterton used to say that pessimists (like the person with that sticker on his car) don't stay anti-life very long when you put a revolver to their heads. All of a sudden, they can think of a million reasons to live. Those million reasons are always there, down inside of us, waiting to be called up. Our pessimism is usually a false front put on to get sympathy.

Another popular bumper sticker has been "Shit Happens." I happen to consider that bumper sticker to be ironically optimistic. It's one of the qualities of optimists that they are not surprised, overwhelmed, or offended by trouble. They know that trouble comes, and they know they can handle it.

Some people have been upset by the popularity of this slogan, and I've seen them try to counter with the sticker, "Love Happens." Actually, they have it wrong. Shit *does* happen. But love does not. Love doesn't happen all by itself. Love is created.

In his stirring book *Son Rise*, Barry Neil Kaufman tells an astonishing true story of how he and his wife healed their once-autistic son and helped nurture him to a happy, extroverted life. Kaufman and his wife made a conscious choice to see their son's disability as a great blessing to them. It was just a choice, like choosing to face the sun instead of facing your shadows. But as Kaufman says, "The way we choose to see the world creates the world we see."

71. Travel deep inside

Most of us wait to find out who we are from impressions and opinions we get from other people. We base our own so-called self-image on other people's views of us.

"Oh, do you really think I'm good at that?" we ask, when someone compliments us. If we're persuaded that they are being honest and have made a good case, we might try to alter our self-image upward.

It's great getting feedback from others, especially positive feedback. We all need it to live and feel good. But when it's all we've got, we're in danger of being far less than we could be, because our *self*-image always depends on *others*. And all they see is what we're risking right now. What they never see is what's inside of us, waiting to emerge. Because they can't see that, they will always underrate us.

Your journey can be internal. You can travel deeper and deeper inside to find out your own potential. Your potential is your true identity—it only waits for self-motivation to come alive.

"For this is the journey that men and women make," said James A. Michener, "to find themselves. If they fail in this, it doesn't matter much else what they find."

Let positive reinforcement and compliments be a mere seasoning to your life. But prepare your life's meal yourself. Don't look outside yourself to *find out* who you are, look inside and *create* who you are.

72. Go to war

Anthony Burgess was 40 when he learned that he had a brain tumor that would kill him within a year. He knew he had a battle on his hands. He was completely broke at the time, and he didn't have anything to leave behind for his wife, Lynne, soon to be a widow.

Burgess had never been a professional novelist in the past, but he always knew the potential was inside him to be a writer. So, for the sole purpose of leaving royalties behind for his wife, he put a piece of paper into a typewriter and began writing. He had no certainty that he would even be published, but he couldn't think of anything else to do.

"It was January of 1960," he said, "and according to the prognosis, I had a winter and spring and summer to live through, and would die with the fall of the leaf."

In that time Burgess wrote energetically, finishing five and a half novels before the year was through—(very nearly the entire lifetime output of E.M. Forster, and almost twice that of J.D. Salinger.)

But Burgess did not die. His cancer had gone into remission and then disappeared altogether. In his long and full life as a novelist (he is best known for *A Clockwork Orange*), he wrote more than 70 books, but without the death sentence from cancer, he may not have written at all.

Many of us are like Anthony Burgess, hiding greatness inside, waiting for some external emergency to bring it out. I believe that's why my father and many people of his generation speak so fondly about World War II. During the war, they lived in a state of emergency that brought out the best in them.

If we don't pay attention to this phenomenon—how crisis inspires our best efforts—we tend to brainlessly create a life based on comfort. We try to design easier and easier ways to live, so that we won't be surprised or challenged by anything.

People who get the knack of self-motivation can reverse this process and get that wonderful "World War II" sense of vitality into their lives. Athletes do it constantly.

"How do you feel about tonight's game with the Trail Blazers?" a reporter once asked basketball star Kobe

Bryant. "It'll be a war out there," he said with a twinkle in his eye.

We don't have to wait for something tragic or dangerous to attack us from the outside. We can get the same vitality going by challenging ourselves from within.

A useful exercise for self-motivation is to ask yourself what you'd do if you had Anthony Burgess's original predicament. "If I had just a year to live, how would I live differently? What exactly would I do?"

73. Use the 5% solution

Many years ago, when I first began considering the idea of changing my life, I went through some emotional mood swings. I would get very high on an idea of who I could be, and I'd set out to change myself overnight. Then my old habits would pull me back to who I used to be, and I would become demoralized and depressed for weeks, thinking I didn't have what it took to change. As the weeks went by, I finally caught on to the idea that great things are often created very slowly, so why couldn't great people be created the same way? I began to see the value in small changes, here and there, that led me in the direction of who I wanted to be.

If I wanted to be someone who was healthy and had good eating habits, I would introduce a salad here, a piece of fruit there, and take the creative process very slowly. Now I almost never eat red meat, but it didn't happen by simply ruling it out one night. (All the times I tried that, my stomach, which used to far outrank my mind in my internal chain of command, would rule it back in the first time I smelled a barbecue in the neighborhood.)

Pyschotherapist Dr. Nathaniel Branden is known for the effectiveness in his therapy of using sentence completion exercises. By asking his clients to write out or speak six to 10 endings, quickly, without thinking, to a "sentence stem," he allows people to explore their own minds for their hidden power and creativity.

A typical sentence he might ask you to complete six to 10 times would be, "If I bring five percent more purposefulness into my life today...."

Then you, the client, give your rapid endings to the sentence. That's how you find out what you think and secretly know about your own power to add purpose to your life. One of the fascinating aspects of Branden's sentences is the "five percent" part. It seems like an awfully small amount of change when you look at it, but think of how it would play out. If you brought five percent more purposefulness to your life each day, it would only be 20 days before you had *doubled* your sense of purpose.

Huge things can be accomplished by focusing on one small action at a time. Novelist Anne Lamott recalls an incident in her childhood, the memory of which always helps her "get a grip."

"Thirty years ago," she remembers, "my older brother, who was 10 years old at the time, was trying to get a report on birds written that he'd had three months to write, which was due the next day. We were out at our family cabin in Bolinas, and he was at the kitchen table close to tears, surrounded by binder paper and pencils and unopened books on birds, immobilized by the hugeness of the task ahead. Then my father sat down beside him, put his arm around my brother's shoulder, and said, 'Bird by bird, buddy. Just take it bird by bird.'"

When we stay the same, it's not because we didn't make a big enough change, but rather because we didn't *do* anything today that sent us moving *toward* change.

If you continue to think of yourself as a great painting you are going to paint, then wanting to instantly change is like wanting to finish your portrait in 10 minutes and then put it up in the art gallery.

If you see yourself as a masterpiece-in-progress, then you will relish small change. A tiny thing you did differently today will excite you. If you want a stronger body, and you took the stairs instead of the elevator, celebrate. You are moving in the direction of change.

If you want to change yourself, try making the changes as small as they can be. If you want to create yourself, like a great painting, don't be afraid to use tiny brush strokes.

74. Do something badly

Sometimes we don't do things because we're not sure we can do them well. We feel that we're not in the mood or at the right energy level to do the task we have to do, so we put it off, or wait for inspiration to arrive.

The most commonly known example of this phenomenon is what writers call "writer's block." A mental barrier seems to set in that prevents a writer from writing. Sometimes it gets so severe that writers go to psychotherapists to get help for it. Many writers' means of earning a living depends on its cure.

The "block" (or lack of self-motivation) occurs not because the writer can't write, but because the writer thinks he can't write *well*. In other words, the writer thinks he doesn't have the proper energy or inspiration to write something, right now, that's good enough to submit. So the pessimistic voice inside the writer says, "You can't think of anything to write, can you?" This happens to many of us, even with something as small as a postcard to send, or an overdue e-mail to answer.

But the writer doesn't really need psychotherapy for this. All he or she needs is an understanding of how the human mind is working at the moment of the "block."

The cure for writer's block—and also the road to self-motivation—is simple. The cure is to go ahead and *write badly*.

Novelist Anne Lamott has a chapter in her marvelous book *Bird by Bird* called "Shitty First Drafts." The key to writing, she says, is to just start typing anything— it can be the worst thing you've ever written, it doesn't matter.

"Almost all good writing begins with terrible first efforts," says Lamott. "You need to start somewhere. Start by getting something—anything—down on paper."

By the mere act of typing you have disempowered the pessimistic "voice" that tried to convince you not to write. Now you are writing. And once you're in action, it's easy to pick up the energy and pick up the quality.

Singer-songwriter John Stewart says, "When you're in the first stages of creating, *never, ever* censor yourself."

We're often afraid to do things until we're sure we'll do them well. Therefore we don't do anything. This tendency led G.K. Chesterton to say, "If a thing is worth doing, it's worth doing badly."

Going out for a run gives me an example of the same phenomenon. Because I don't feel that I have a good, strong run in me, the voice says "not today." But the cure for that is to decide to do it anyway—even if it will be a bad run. "I don't feel like running now, so I'm going to go out and run slowly, in such lazy, bad form that it does me no good, but at least I will have run."

But once I start, something always happens to alter my feelings about the run. By the end of the run, I notice that it had somehow become thoroughly enjoyable.

In my self-motivation seminars, I often give a homework assignment for people to write down what their main goals are for the next year. I ask them to fill no more than a half-page. This is not a difficult assignment for people who are willing to just come off the top of their heads and have fun filling the page. But you would be surprised at how many people absolutely anguish over it, trying to get it "right," as if they were going to be held forever to what they write down. Many people simply can't do it.

To get them to complete the exercise, I say, "put anything down. Make something up. It doesn't even have to be true. They don't even have to be *your* goals, just do it so you can understand the exercise we're about to do." The point is to just do it.

In many ways we are all novelists like Anne Lamott. Our novels are our lives. And many of us get a tragic form of writer's block that causes us to not write anything at all. It's a tragedy, because deep down we are very creative. We could write a great life. It's just that we're so afraid of writing badly, that we never write.

Don't let this happen to you. If you're not motivated to do something you know you need to do, just decide to do it badly. Add a little self-deprecating humor. Be comically bad at what you're doing. And then enjoy what happens to you once you're into the process.

75. Learn visioneering

A few years ago I spent some enjoyable time working with motivational speaker Dennis Deaton and teaching his principles of "visioneering"—which he defines as "engineering dreams into reality" by the use of active mental imaging.

When I gave my weekly Thursday night public seminars, I'd sometimes teach Deaton's "visioneering" concepts, and my (then) little daughter Margery would always accompany me. She helped hand out workbooks and pencils and when the seminar got started she would take a seat in the audience, open her own workbook and participate. She was 10 at the time, and I was never certain exactly how much she was absorbing.

Then one weekend afternoon by the pool at our apartment complex, I relaxed in a deck chair while Margie and her girlfriend Michelle played by the pool. There were a lot of people in and around the water that day, but above them all I could hear Margery and Michelle having a heated conversation down by the deep end of the water.

"I just can't do it!" said Michelle.

"Yes, you can," said Margie. "You just have to believe you can."

"I'm *afraid* to dive," said Michelle. "I've never dived in my life."

"Michelle," said Margie, "listen to me. Will you just try it my way?"

"I don't know," said Michelle. "Okay, what's your way?"

"Just close your eyes," said Margie, "and picture yourself on a diving board. Can you see yourself standing up there?"

"Yes," said Michelle.

"Okay good!" said Margie. "Now, I want you to get an even better picture. What kind of bathing suit are you wearing? Can you see it?"

"It's red, white, and blue," said Michelle, her eyes still closed. "It's like an American flag."

"Great," said Margie. "Now picture yourself diving off the board in slow motion, just like in a dream. Can you see that?"

"Yes I can," said Michelle.

"That's great!" shouted Margie. "Now you can do it. Because if you can dream it, you can do it! Let's go over here and do it."

Michelle followed her slowly to the end of the pool. I was looking over the top of my book but not letting them know I was listening. I was amazed. I had no idea what would happen next, but I noticed a number of people around the pool area watching and listening with fascination, while pretending not to.

Michelle walked up to the edge of the water and looked very scared. She looked at Margie, and Margie said, "Michelle, I want you to keep saying, very softly, 'If I can dream it, I can do it' and then I want to see you dive in."

Michelle kept repeating "If I can dream it, I can do it," and all of a sudden, surprising even herself, she dove—a near-perfect dive into the deep end with almost no splash!

Margie was jumping up and down and clapping when Michelle came up from the water. "You did it!" she shouted, and Michelle was grinning as she climbed up to do it again.

Could it be, I thought to myself, that this system is this simple?

The principle is this: You won't do anything you can't picture yourself doing. Visioneering is just another word for picturing yourself. Once you make the picturing process conscious and deliberate, you begin to create the self you want to be. We dive into the pictures we create.

76. Lighten things up

Sunlight and laughter. That's what cures most fears and worries. Terrifying problems are better solved in the light than in the dark. And there are many ways to bring them into the light.

Pick a frightening problem. Then do the following: Talk about it with someone, draw an illustrated map of it on a huge piece of paper, make "Top 10" lists about the problem, tell yourself some jokes about the problem, sing about the problem and, finally, dance a dance that expresses the problem.

If you do all these things, I promise you that your problem will seem a lot funnier, and less frightening, than it once did. It is impossible to laugh deeply and be frightened at the same time.

G.K Chesterton used to say that "taking things lightly" was the most spiritually advanced thing you could do to improve your effectiveness in life.

"After all," said Chesterton; "it's because God's angels take themselves so lightly that they are able to fly. And if His angels take themselves that lightly, imagine how much *more* lightly He takes Himself."

My friend Fred Knipe is a three-time Emmy award-winning television writer who also performs as a comedian in the character of "Dr. M.F. Ludiker"—world expert on everything. Fred is one of the funniest human beings I have ever known. He never fails to lighten me up, no matter how big the problem I have.

Dr. Ludiker mounts the stage and puts his ludicrous "Ludiker Institute" logo in front of the podium—a logo that features a cartoon human brain hanging between two electrical towers. He then proceeds to give, in a mild Teutonic accent, his "advice from hell."

"With the increase in domestic violence," the doctor says, "I am advocating that home appliance manufacturers begin installing airbags."

On the subject of our growing intolerance of crime, he says—"Criminals, among the most deeply tense in our communities, will soon have trouble recruiting top people because they can no longer escape the sense that there is resentment building about what they do for a living."

"It was inevitable," he observes, "that genetic engineering would come from a generation that played Mr. Potato Head."

Knipe's editing of my writing also causes me to lighten up. (While making helpful handwritten notes on the manuscript for this book, he recommended that I refer to the Lakota shaman Lame Deer as "Super Shaman Lame Deer.")

While going through my recovery from a frightening disease that featured, at one point, uncontrolled bleeding, he left me a comforting phone message that said, "Don't worry about the bleeding. It's normal for someone your age."

Fred shares my long-held belief that humor is the highest form of creativity. It's the hardest to produce and the most enjoyable to receive. Humor, like all other creativity, is a matter of making unusual combinations. The more surprising the combination, the funnier the humor.

Your own motivational level will always be lifted by humor. Any time you are stuck, ask yourself to take things lightly. Ask yourself to come up with some funny solutions. Laughter will destroy all limits to your thinking. When you are laughing, you are open to anything.

77. Serve and grow rich

One good way to motivate yourself is by increasing the flow of money into your life.

Most people are embarrassed to even think this way. They don't want to "think and grow rich" because they think they will be thought of as selfish or greedy. Or maybe they still believe in the thoroughly discredited Marxist economic superstition that to make money, you have to take it away from somebody else. Or else they don't want to come across as being obsessed with money.

But do you know who is *really* obsessed with money? People who don't have any. They obsess about money all day long. It's in their family discussions, it's in their minds at night, and it becomes a destructive part of their relationships during the day.

The best way *not* to be obsessed with money is to trust your game plan for earning your way to financial freedom. "Our first duty," said George Bernard Shaw, "is not to be poor."

The road to not being poor always travels through your professional relationships in life. The more you serve those relationships, the more productive those relationships will become, and the more money you will make.

"Money is life energy that we exchange and use as a result of the service we provide to the universe," wrote Deepak Chopra in *Creating Affluence.* When you understand that money flows from service, you have a chance to understand something even more valuable: Unexpectedly large amounts of money come from *unexpectedly large degrees of service.*

The way to generate unexpected service to the people in your life is to ask yourself, "What do they *expect?*" Once you're clear on what that is, then ask, "What can I do that they would not expect?" It's always the unexpected service that gets talked about. And it's always getting talked about that increases your professional value.

As Napoleon Hill repeatedly pointed out, great wealth comes from the habit of going the extra mile. And it is always a smart business move to do a little more than you are paid for.

It is almost impossible to enjoy a life of self-motivation when you're worried about money. Don't be embarrassed about giving this subject a great deal of thought. Thinking about money a little bit in advance frees you from having to always think about it later. Allow yourself to link financial well-being with an increased capacity for compassion for others. If I am living in poverty, how much love and attention can I give to my children or my fellow humans? How much help can I be if I, for sheer lack of creative planning, am always worried about being in debt?

"Poverty is no disgrace," said Napoleon Hill. "But it is certainly not a recommendation."

78. Make a list of your life

Never hesitate to sit down with yourself and make lists. The more you write things down, the more you can dictate your own future. There is an unfortunate myth that lists make things trivial. But lists do the opposite—they make things come alive.

I have a friend who made a list of all the positive things about himself that he could think of. He listed every characteristic and accomplishment that he could remember in his life that he was proud of. He keeps the list in his briefcase, and says he often reads through it when he's feeling down.

"By seeing all those things written down, and letting myself read them one at a time, I can change my entire attitude from being discouraged to feeling positive about myself," he says.

Writing lists of goals and objectives is also a powerful self-motivator. It's one thing to go into a meeting mentally briefed on what you want to accomplish, but you'll feel even stronger having written it out. There is something about writing something down that makes it more real to the right side of your brain.

My friend Fred Knipe sometimes travels to Phoenix to spend a day talking with me. We've been close friends since college and share an unorthodox sense of humor. Our meetings together are anything but structured. We free-associate and talk about everything under the sun.

Yet, I notice that he'll often arrive with a list.

In the days prior to our meeting, he'll jot down subjects he wants to be sure he remembers to talk to me about while we are together. And it's *because* our conversations are so free-form that the list is valuable for him. He doesn't ever have to call me back the next day and try to discuss something over the phone that would have been much better discussed in person.

If you've ever tried grocery shopping for a large event without a shopping list, you are aware of the nightmare it can be. Most people have learned not to shop that way. I've learned by hard experience that it can mean additional trips to the store to pick up forgotten items.

Yet why is it that people don't apply that same principle to their lives? Most people take more time planning a picnic than they do planning a life. Because they *know* that if they don't make a list and forget the hot dog buns as a result, they are going to be called an idiot by someone.

But isn't a life as important as a picnic?

Start by listing all the things you would like to do before you die. Keep the list somewhere handy, where you can look at it and add to it.

Then list the people in your life you want to remain close to and stay in touch with. Friendship is so precious, why let it be forgotten? It sounds silly to make a list of your friends, but you'll be surprised at how it reminds you who's important and motivates you to stay in touch.

My friend Terry Hill, the writer, is one of the greatest list-makers of all time. He has a list of every book he has ever read, every poem he's read, and many more things I don't even know about. It gives his life a sense of history, depth, and direction.

We don't have to wait to become famous so that someone else might write our history. We can be writing our history while it happens.

And when we list our goals, we're writing our history *before* it happens. When legendary advertising executive David Ogilvy started his advertising agency, by making a list of the clients that he most wanted—General Foods, Lever Brothers, Bristol Myers, Campbell Soup Company, and Shell Oil. At the time, they were the biggest advertising accounts in the world, and he had none of them. But in a sense he did have them, because they were in his list.

"It took time," said Ogilvy, "but in due course I got them all."

A goal gains power when you write it down, and more power *every time you write it down.*

What motivates you most in life ought to be in your own handwriting. People all too often look for motivation in what others have written. If you become a good list-maker, you will learn how to motivate yourself by what *you've* written.

79. Set a specific power goal

Most people are surprised to learn that the reason they're not getting what they want in life is because their goals are too small. And too vague. And therefore have no power.

Your goals will never be reached if they fail to excite your imagination. What really excites the imagination is the setting of a large and specific *power* goal.

Usually, a goal is just a goal. But a *power goal* is a goal that takes on a huge reality. It lives and breathes. It provides motivational energy. It gets you up in the morning. You can taste it, smell it, and feel it. You've got it clearly pictured in your mind. You've got it written down. And you love writing it down because every time you do it fills you with clarity of purpose.

In his audiotape series, "Visioneering," my old partner Dennis Deaton teaches the transforming power of lofty goals. Deaton talks about creating a "mental movie" that you watch as often as possible. He urges you to make it a movie that stars *you*—living the results of achieving your specific goal.

Walt Disney left us many great things: Disneyland, Walt Disney World, great animated films, and Annette Funicello. But what I believe was his greatest gift was the summing up he did of his life's work: "If you can dream it," he said, "you can do it."

A power goal is a dream with a deadline. The deadline itself motivates you. People who have created power goals start living on purpose. They know what they're up to in life.

How can you tell if you've got a big enough and real enough power goal? Simply observe the effect your goal has on you. It's not what a goal *is* that matters; it's what a goal *does*.

80. Change yourself first

Don't change other people. It doesn't work. You'll waste your life trying.

Many of us spend all our time trying to change the people in our lives. We think we can change them in ways that will make them better equipped to make us happy. This is especially true of our children. We talk to our children for hours about how we think they should change. But children don't learn from what we say. They learn from what we do.

Today's children, upon hearing us talk to them about how they should change will often say, "Yeah, right." I think they got this phrase from Bart Simpson. It's shorthand for "I'm not listening to what you say, I'm listening to what you do."

Gandhi was especially tuned in to the futility of changing other people. Yet Gandhi was probably responsible for more change in people than any other person in our era was. How did he do it? He had a profoundly simple formula. People would often come to Gandhi to ask how they could change others. Someone would say, "I agree with you about nonviolence, but there are others who don't. How do I change them?" And Gandhi told them they couldn't. He said you couldn't change other people.

"You must *be* the change you wish to see in others," said Gandhi. In my own seminars, I probably use that one quotation more than any other. I am always asked,

"How can I change my husband?" Or, "How can I change my wife?" Or, "How can I change my teenager?"

People who take the seminars on self-motivation, at some point during the workshop, agree completely with the principles and ideas. Then, they start to think about the people who *don't* buy in. In the question-and-answer period, their questions are about *those poor people*. How do we change *them*? I always quote Gandhi. *Be* the change you wish to see in others.

By *being* what you want *them* to be, you lead by inspiration. Nobody really wants to be taught by lectures and advice. They want to be led through inspiration.

Sales managers often ask me how they can get a certain salesperson to do more self-motivated activities. I tell them that they have to *be* the salesperson they want to see. Take them on a call, I say, and let them watch you. Don't tell them how to do it, inspire them to do it.

I once attended a concert given by my daughter's fourth-grade chorus, which sang a song called "Let There Be Peace on Earth." The song's words went, "Let there be peace on earth, *and let it begin with me....*" I beamed when I heard it. It was such a beautiful expression of *being the change*—a celebration of self-responsibility that rarely is portrayed in young people's lives today.

What you *tell* people to do often goes right by them. Who you *are* does not.

81. Pin your life down

Car dealer extraordinaire Henry Brown once told me a story about his son, a high school wrestler. His boy had been getting only fair results as a wrestler that year and when Henry talked to him about it he learned the reason.

Henry's son entered each wrestling match more than thoroughly prepared to *counter* anything his opponent tried.

But no matter how gifted Henry's son was at countering moves, countering was still countering, so the other wrestler always dictated the tempo. Finally, Henry suggested to his son that he try entering a wrestling match with his own attack *plan*—a series of moves that *he* would initiate no matter what his opponent tried.

The boy agreed, and the results were remarkable. He began winning match after match, pinning opponent after opponent.

The young wrestler's goal had always been to win. He didn't have a problem setting goals. But what had to be added was a plan of action. In sports, as in life, goals alone aren't always enough. As Nathaniel Branden says, "A goal without an action plan is a daydream."

Henry Brown didn't just give that advice to his son because he bought into it theoretically. His own Brown and Brown Chevrolet dealership has many times been the number one Chevy dealership in the nation because he plans his company's own yearly performance in the same way he coached his son.

Every year he has his general manager send me the detailed videotape that outlines the dealership's game plan for the coming year. It includes all the department's projected earnings down to the penny. By boldly charting such a specific course, Brown lets the market *respond to him*. Once, when I asked him how his dealership got through a previous year's nationwide automotive sales recession he said, "We decided not to participate in it."

Before any adventure, take time to plan. Design your own plan of attack. Don't just counter what some other wrestler is doing. Let life respond to *you*. If you're making all the first moves, you'll be surprised at how often you can pin life down.

82. Take no for a question

Don't take *no* for an answer. Take it for a question. Make the word *no* mean this question: "Can't you be more creative than that?"

In my seminars I work with a lot of salespeople and one of the most requested topics of discussion is "cold-calling and rejection." One of the greatest problems salespeople, and people everywhere, face is in the meaning *they give* to someone else's *no*. Many people hear *no* as an absolute, final, and devastating personal rejection. But *no* can mean anything you want it to mean.

When I graduated from college with a degree in English, I was not overwhelmed with companies trying to hire me. Most people already speak English. So I decided to try to get a job as a sports writer at the daily evening paper in Tucson, Arizona, *The Tucson Citizen*. I had spent four years in the army, and I hadn't done any sportswriting since high school.

When I applied for the job, I was told that my major problem was that I had never done any professional sportswriting before. It was the typical situation of a company not being able to hire you because you haven't had experience—but how can you gain experience if no one will hire you?

My first impulse was to take *no* to be their final answer. After all, that's what they said it was. But I finally decided to have *no* mean—"Can't you be more creative than that?"

So I went home to think and plot my next move. The reason they wouldn't hire me was because I had no experience. When I asked them why that was important, they smiled and said, "We have no way of knowing for sure whether you can write sports. Just being an English major isn't enough."

Then it hit me. Their real problem wasn't my lack of experience—it was *their lack of knowledge.* They didn't know whether I could write well enough. So I set out to solve their problem for them. I began to write them letters. I knew they were interviewing four other people for the position and that they would decide within a month. Every day I wrote a letter to the sports editor, the late Regis McAuley (an award-winning writer in his own right, who made his reputation in Cleveland before coming to Tucson).

My letters were long and expressive. I made them as creative and clever as I could, commenting on the sports news of the day, and letting them know how great a fit I thought I was for their staff.

After a month, Mr. McAuley called me and said that they had narrowed it down to two candidates, and I was one of them. Would I come in for a final interview? I was so excited, I nearly swallowed the phone.

When my interview was coming to an end (I was the second one in), McAuley had one last question for me.

"Let me ask you something, Steve," he said. "If we hire you, will you promise that you'll stop sending me those endless letters?"

I said I would stop, and then he laughed and said, "Then you're hired. You can start Monday."

McAuley later told me that the letters did the trick.

"First of all, they showed me that you could write," he said. "And second of all, they proved to me that you wanted the position more than the other candidates did."

When you ask for something in professional life and it is denied to you, imagine that the *no* you heard is really a question: "Can't you be more creative than that?" Never accept *no* at face value. Let rejection motivate you to get more creative.

83. Take the road to somewhere

Energy comes from purpose. If the left side of your brain tells the right side of your brain that there's a sufficient crisis, the right side sends you energy, sometimes superhuman energy.

That's why there's such a difference between people who set and achieve goals all day, and people who just do whatever comes up, or whatever they feel like doing. To one person, there is always added purpose. To the other, there is boredom and confusion, the two greatest robbers of energy.

Knowing what you're up to, and why you're up to it, gives you the energy to self-motivate. Not knowing your purpose drains you of all motivation.

We've all heard the stories of the diminutive mother who, seeing that her small child was trapped, lifted a tremendously heavy object, such as a car, so the child could be freed. When asked to repeat the superhuman feat later, of course the woman couldn't do it.

Being a single father has put me in touch with the dramatic connection between purpose and energy. If I am cooking something, for example, and out of the corner of my eye I can see flames emerging from the kitchen, it is amazing how fast I can move from the living room into the kitchen. Crisis creates instant purpose, which creates instant energy.

The "He ain't heavy, he's my brother" idea is based on purpose. When our purpose is great, so is our strength and energy.

"But, I don't know what my purpose is," a lot of people tell me, as if someone forgot to tell them what it is. Those people may wait forever to be told how to live and what to live for.

There can only be two reasons why you don't know your purpose: 1) you don't talk to yourself; and 2) you don't know where purpose comes from. (You think purpose comes from outside yourself instead of from within.)

Purposeful people know how to go deep into their own spirit and talk to themselves about why they exist, and what they want to do with the gift of life.

"Only human beings have come to a point where they no longer know why they exist," said the Lakota shaman Lame Deer. "They don't use their brains and they have forgotten the secret knowledge of their bodies, their senses, or their dreams."

Lame Deer is not optimistic about what the future holds for people who live without purpose.

"They don't use the knowledge the spirit has put into every one of them," he says. "They are not even aware of this, and so they stumble along blindly on the road to nowhere—a paved highway that they themselves bulldoze and make smooth so that they can get faster to the big empty hole that they'll find at the end, waiting to swallow them up. It's a quick, comfortable superhighway, but I know where it leads. I've seen it. I've been there in my vision and it makes me shudder to think about it."

Purpose can be built, strengthened, and made more inspiring every day. We are totally responsible for our own sense of purpose. We can go inside our own spirit and create it, or not. The energy of our lives is wholly dependent on how much purpose we're willing to create.

84. Go on a news fast

I first heard the phrase "news fast" from Dr. Andrew Weil, who writes about natural medicine and spontaneous healing. Weil recommends going on news fasts because he believes this has a healing effect on the human system. To him, it's a genuine health issue.

My own recommendation for news fasts has to do with the psychology of self-motivation. If you go for periods of time without listening to or reading the news, you will notice an upswing in your optimism about life. You'll feel a lift in energy.

"But shouldn't I stay informed?" people ask me. "Aren't I being a bad citizen if I don't keep up with what's happening in my community? Shouldn't I be watching the news?"

In answer to this question, I offer an observation that may startle you: The news is no longer the news.

It used to be that Walter Cronkite would end his program by saying, "And that's the way it is." And we trusted that he was right. But today, it's much different. Shock value has the highest premium of all for a news story, and the lines are now blurred between the evening news and the grossest tabloids. Tom Brokaw is as likely to lead his show with a story about a woman cutting off her husband's private parts as is *The National Enquirer.*

Today, the goal of the person putting the evening news show together is to stimulate our emotions in as many ways as possible. Every night we will see human suffering. We will also see con artists, and even whole companies getting away with scams that victimize people cruelly. If there's a report on politics, it features the most venomous attacks between two partisans.

The goal of the news today is stimulation. It's to take us on an emotional roller-coaster ride. It's a "good" program if we have been enraged by one story, saddened by another, and amused by at the third.

Is it any wonder that by programming our minds with this gross and frightening information all day and into the night, we end up a little less motivated? Is it hard to understand a certain slippage in our optimism?

Going on a news fast is a refreshing cure for this problem. You can do it for one day a week, to begin with, and then get back into the tabloid shows the next day if you have to. Once you start fasting, you'll find your entire mood picking up.

"But what about staying informed?" you ask. There are many ways to stay fully informed. The Internet has wonderful, thoughtful sites. In fact, it is far better to be informed intellectually than to be informed emotionally. There are weekly and monthly magazines as well as e-zines that do a fine job of informing us and giving us a calm, thoughtful, overall perspective of the news.

Don't worry about missing out on important news. Really big news, like a war, a natural disaster, or an assassination will get to you just as quickly during a news fast as it would if you were watching the news.

Begin to experiment with news fasts today. Go on a short one at first, and then extend the periods of time as your system allows. When you *do* return to the news, be totally conscious of just what the show is trying to do to you. Don't passively take it in as if what you are seeing is really "the way it is." It's not. They're not going to tell you how many thousands of planes landed safely today.

85. Replace worry with action

Don't worry. Or rather, don't just worry. Let worry change into action. When you find yourself worrying about something, ask yourself the action question, "What can I *do* about this right now?"

And then do something. Anything. Any small thing.

Most of my life, I spent my time asking myself the wrong question every time I worried. I asked myself, "What should I be feeling about this?" I finally discovered that I was much happier when I started asking, instead, "What can I *do* about this?"

If I am worried about the conversation I had with my wife last night, and how unfair I might have been to say the things I said, I can ask myself, "What can I *do* about that right now?"

By putting the question into the *action* arena, a lot of possibilities will occur to me: 1) I could send her flowers; or 2) I could call her to tell her I was concerned about how I left things; or 3) I could leave a nice little note somewhere for her; or 4) I could go see her to make things right. All of these possibilities are actions, and when I act on something, the worry goes away.

We often hear the phrase "worry it to death." But that phrase doesn't reflect what really happens when we worry. It would be great if we *could* worry something to death. When it dies, we could dispose of the body and be done with it.

But when we worry, we don't worry a thing to death, we worry it *to life*. Our worrying makes the problem grow. And most of the time, we worry it into a grotesque kind of life, a kind of Frankenstein's monster that frightens us beyond all reason.

I once came up with a system for action that helped turn my worrying habits completely around. I would list the five things that I was worried about—perhaps they were four projects at work and the fifth was my son's trouble he was having with a certain teacher. I would then decide to spend *five minutes* on each problem doing something, anything. By deciding this, I knew I was committing myself to 25 minutes of activity. No more. So it didn't feel at all overwhelming.

Then I could make a game of it. On project one, a seminar workbook deadline for a new course, I'd spend five minutes writing it. Maybe I only got the first two pages done, but it felt great. It felt like I'd finally started it.

Then on item number two, a meeting I knew I had to have with a client over a sticky contract issue, I would call his office and schedule the meeting and put it in my calendar. That, too, felt good.

My third worry, a stack of correspondence I needed to answer, I would take five minutes sorting and stacking and putting them into a folder that was separate from the other clutter on my desk. That felt satisfying, too. The fourth item was a travel arrangement that had to be worked out. I'd take no more than five minutes looking at my calendar and leaving a voice mail for my travel agent to fax me some alternatives on the trip.

Finally, on the matter of my son, I would pull out a piece of paper and write a short letter to his teacher expressing my concern for him, my support of her efforts, and my desire to arrange a meeting quickly, so all three of us could sit down together and make some agreements.

All of that took 25 minutes. And the five things that were worrying me the most were no longer worrying me. I could then go back anytime later and work them to completion.

If something is worrying you, always *do* something about it. It doesn't have to be the big thing that will make it disappear. It can be any small thing. But the positive effect it will have on you will be enormous.

A friend of mine was worried about her cat, which had some mild symptoms of illness, but nothing that looked severe enough to take the cat to the veterinarian. She also thought the symptoms were so subtle that they might not be easy to describe to the vet, but still she worried. She brought the subject up two or three more times before I finally said to her, "You must do something."

"That's just the problem, there's nothing to do," she said.

"Take some kind of action," I said. "Call the vet and talk to him."

"That doesn't make sense because the vet wouldn't know anything from what I told him, and he'd probably ask me to take her in to see him, and I know it's not that serious," she said.

"Yes, I understand," I said, "But you should take the action for *you*, not for the cat or the vet. By not doing anything you're keeping yourself trapped in worrying."

"Okay," she said. "I see what you mean."

When she called the vet, to her surprise, the vet was able to make a good assessment of what was wrong. He recommended that she bring the cat in, and if it was what he thought it was, he could give her something to clear it up right away.

Anything that worries you should be *acted on,* not just thought about. Don't be scared about the action; you can make it very small and easy, as long as you take an action. Even small actions will chase away your fears. Fear has a hard time coexisting with action. When there's action, there's no fear. When there's fear, there's no action.

The next time you're worried about something, ask yourself, "What small thing can I do right now?" Then do it. Remember not to ask, "What could I possibly do to make this whole thing go away?" That question does not get you into action at all.

Acting on your worries frees you up for other things. It removes fear and uncertainty from your life and puts you back in control of creating what you want. Just do it.

86. Run with the thinkers

The president of a major office equipment company put his problem to me this way: "How do I get the whiners in my company to stop whining and start coming up with solutions?"

He went on to explain that he had two kinds of people working for him, the Whiners and the Thinkers.

The Whiners were often very smart and dedicated employees who worked long, hard hours. But when they came into the manager's office, it was almost always to complain.

"They're great at finding fault with other managers and telling me what's wrong with our systems," the president said, "but they are a drain on me because they're so negative that I end up trying to make them feel better. After that, I'm depressed."

The Thinkers, on the other hand, had a different way of coming into the office with problems.

"The Thinkers come to me with ideas," he said. "They see the same problems that the Whiners see, but they've already thought about possible solutions."

The Thinkers, in other words, have assumed ownership of the company, and are creating the future of the company with their thinking. The Whiners have stopped thinking. Once the problems are identified, and their reaction to them justified, the thinking stops.

The Thinkers have taken their reaction to the company's problems past their emotions, and into their minds. And because they have formulated some solutions, the nature of their meeting with the manager is creative. It's a brainstorming meeting. The manager enjoys these meetings because they stimulate his mind, too. Both parties leave the meeting feeling energized intellectually, and the manager looks forward to future meetings with the Thinkers.

The Whiners have left their reaction to their company's problems down at the emotional level. They express resentment, fear, and worry. The manager's problem in such a meeting is that he deals primarily with those emotions, so he finishes the meeting with his own sense of discouragement.

When you are committed to self-motivation as a way of life, you will fall into the realm of the Thinker. Your thinking not only creates your motivation, but it creates your relationships, your family, and the organization you work for as well, because they are all a part of you. You are more valuable to your organization with this orientation to thinking, and you're more valuable to yourself.

87. Put more enjoyment in

There is a huge difference between pleasure and enjoyment. And when we're absolutely clear about the difference, we can grow much faster toward a focused and energized life.

Mihaly Csikszentmihalyi best describes this difference in his various books on "flow"—the psychological state that we get in when time disappears and we are thoroughly engaged in what we're doing.

Csikszentmihalyi distinguishes what we do for pleasure (routine sex, eating, drinking, etc.) from what we do for enjoyment. Enjoyment is deeper. Enjoyment always involves the use of a skill and the facing of a challenge. So sailing, gardening, painting, bowling, golfing, cooking, and any such activity involving skills meeting a challenge constitute enjoyment.

People who get clear on that difference begin to put more enjoyment into their lives. They reach the happy and fulfilled psychological state known as "flow." Increasing their skills and seeking challenges to engage those skills are what lead to an enjoyable life.

There are many stories and accounts about the winners of lotteries who are jubilant when they win, but whose lives descend into a nightmare after acquiring that *unearned* money. (No challenge, no skill.) The lottery looks like "the answer" to people because they associate money with pleasure. But the true enjoyment of money comes in part from the *earning* of it, which involves skill and challenge.

Watching television is usually done for pleasure. That's why so few people can remember (or make use of) any of the 30 hours of television they have watched in the past week. In watching television, there is no combination of skill and challenge.

Contrast that dull pleasure hangover we get from watching television with what happens when we spend the same amount of time preparing for a big Thanksgiving dinner for friends and relatives. In looking back, we remember quite vividly the entire Thanksgiving endeavor.

Despite her run-ins with Wall Street and the law, one of the most intriguing people on our national scene has always been Martha Stewart. Throughout the 1990s, she personified mastery of the concept of small enjoyments. Her magazines and television programs celebrated cooking, gardening, and home entertainment skills. Her own contagious enthusiasm for the things she enjoyed made her, in my opinion, one of that era's true heroes of optimism. If you're feeling like you have forgotten how to *enjoy* your own home, yard, or kitchen, you might buy one of her books and allow her optimism to inspire you.

You can increase your own self-motivation by learning to be more aware of the profound difference between enjoyment and mere pleasure.

88. Keep walking

Ever since I was a child, I had a recurring dream that I began each day facing a mattress. The more I pushed into this mattress before my day began, the more the indentation went in, and the more saved-up the sprung energy of the mattress got. The more the mattress was indented with my pushing at the start of the day, the higher it would spring up when I lay down on it to sleep at night.

I would lie down on this mattress at night and see how high my dreams would fly me. How high I flew would always depend on the indentations I gave the mattress during the day. The impressions I gave it. How impressive I was. The difference I made.

So then after thinking about that dream the other day I decided to step up my walking. I decided that the recurring dream was the way my subconscious chose to tell me something vital. Something about the difference walking made. Something about oxygen being pushed into my system.

Walking would be an action I could take while wide-awake. Walking would drive more oxygen into my lungs.

I would become more like the great football coach Amos Alonzo Stagg, who lived to be 103 years old. Amos Alonzo Stagg was asked how he lived to be so old (the average life expectancy during his lifetime was 65) and he said, "I have, for the greater part of my life, indulged in running and other vigorous exercise that forced large amounts of oxygen into my body."

I increased my walking just to see what would happen if my lungs became my mattress. I began to get happier. I began to enjoy life more. I began to be more *motivated*.

As I walked, I wondered: What if the spirit lives as an aura around us? What if the spirit were a cloud of energy that exists around and outside our bodies ready at all times to be breathed in? Drawn right into the soul?

What if when you breathed deeply, you pulled in your own spirit? And you received energy for action— energy for an explosive take-down of one of your out-of-control problems.

What if the solution to problems outside you was inside you?

Deepak Chopra quotes an ancient anonymous Indian sage as identifying humanity's near-fatal superstition: "You believe that you live in the universe when in reality the universe lives in you."

Many modern scientific books are now referring to the human brain as the "three-pound universe." When the body moves, so does the mind. So does that inner world. When you're walking, you are organizing your mind whether you want to be or not.

Soon we realize that the mind and the body *are* connected. When the Greeks said the secret to a happy life was a sound mind in a sound body, they were on to a powerful truth.

I try to talk myself *out* of that truth many times a week. I'm too tired to exercise. I have an injury. I haven't had enough sleep. I should listen to my body! I would be short-changing my children of the important time they need with me if I selfishly went out for my long walk.

But I am always better off if I choose the walk. I am even better at relating to my children, because walking takes me to the soul.

That's why I can't leave it out. I can't pretend it has nothing to do with this subject, because it's how I pull the truth to me. I pull the globe around toward me under my feet by walking. As the world turns, the lies leak out of my mind, into space. As the body becomes sound, so does the mind. It's true.

And the songs in my head keep the rhythm of the walk going: Fats Domino. Ricky Nelson. Ten Years After. I'm walkin'. Yes indeed. I'm goin' home.

There is something about walking that combines opposites. Opposites: activity and relaxation. (This very paradox is what creates whole-brain thinking.) Opposites: out in the world and solitude. (Alone, but out there walking.)

This combining of opposites activates the harmony I need between the right and left brain, between the adult and the child, between the higher self and the animal. Great solutions appear. Truth becomes beauty.

You have your own walking available to you, too. Yes indeed. It might be dancing or swimming or running or racquetball or boxing or aerobics, but it's all the same thing. It's all a way of moving the body around like a merry plaything and oxygenating the spirit in the process.

89. Read more mysteries

My great friend and editor Kathy Eimers, to whom I first dedicated this book, and later married, has always been a devoted reader of mystery novels. When I first met her, I thought, "How curious that someone so intelligent would be reading mystery novels all the time."

It was especially interesting to me because Kathy is one of the most literate people I'd ever met, a quick thinker and a skilled professional writer and editor. Her editing of my books had been the one thing, in my opinion, that gave them the sparkle that people said they enjoyed.

In my own ignorance, I assumed mystery novels were pretty light fare. Hardly a challenge to the human mind. Now I've begun to change my mind. Not only am I peeking into some of the mystery books she has recommended (I've enjoyed Agatha Christie and Colin Dexter), but I've begun to find out more about what good mystery does to the intellectual energy of the human mind.

Kathy has one of the most creative and energetic problem-solving minds I've ever encountered. I constantly marvel at her mental energy and perception because it stays clear and sharp—all day, and long into the night. I would often find my own mental acuity descending the evolutionary ladder as night approached, while hers stayed alive and creative.

The person with the highest IQ ever measured— Marilyn Vos Savant—recommends mystery novels as brain builders.

"Not only is this exercise fun, but it's good for you," she says. "I'm not talking about violent thrillers, or police procedural novels, but instead I'm directing you to those elegant, clue-filled, intelligent mysteries solved by drawing conclusions, not guns."

Vos Savant sees the reading of mysteries as something that leads to a stronger intelligence.

"If you try to keep one step ahead of the detective in an Agatha Christie or a Josephine Tey or a P.D. James mystery novel, it will sharpen your intuition," she writes in *Brain Building*. "The Sherlock Holmes stories by Arthur Conan Doyle never go out of favor, and rightly so. Holmes's methods are brain-builders brought to life."

When people think of personal transformation, they don't normally think they can strengthen their own intelligence. IQ is something our cultural attitudes have always said we're born with and stuck with. But Vos Savant, whose IQ was measured at 230 (the average adult IQ is 100), believes strongly that the brain can be built as surely and as quickly as the muscles of the body.

So the next time you feel like curling up with a good mystery, don't feel guilty or nonproductive. It might be the most productive thing you've done all day.

90. Think your way up

In some of my seminars I like to draw a picture of a ladder on the board and call it "the ladder of selves."

On the very bottom I write "The Physical," in the middle I put "The Emotional," and at the top I place "The Mind." We can move up or down this ladder by the sheer force of will, although most people don't know they have that option.

By traveling up the ladder, past the physical, through the emotional, and into your mind, you have the opportunity to be creative and thoughtful. You can see possibilities.

Many of us, however, never get past the emotional section of the ladder. When we're stuck there, we begin thinking with our feelings instead of thinking with our minds.

If you hurt my feelings, and I'm angry and resentful, I might give you a long and eloquent speech about what's wrong with you and how you operate. But, because I'm thinking with my feelings instead of my mind, I'm destroying something with my speech instead of creating an understanding.

People do this without knowing it. They let their emotions speak for them, instead of their thoughts. So what you hear is fear, anger, sadness, or other emotions put to words, but never creating anything.

If you can picture this ladder inside of you, and start to notice that you are letting your feelings do your thinking and speaking, you can move up. You can get creative and really think and *then* speak. As Emmet Fox says, "Love is always creative and fear is always destructive."

Go ahead and feel your feelings. But when it's time to talk, let your mind into the conversation. Your mind is what motivates you to your highest performance, not your feelings.

91. Exploit your weakness

Make a list of your strengths and your weaknesses on separate pieces of paper. Place the list of strengths somewhere where you'll see it again, because it will always pick you up.

Now look at your list of weaknesses and study them for a while. Stay with them until you feel no shame or guilt about them. Allow them to become interesting characteristics, instead of negative traits. Ask yourself how each characteristic could be useful to you. That's not what we usually ask about our weaknesses, but that's my whole point.

When I was a boy I remember watching a remarkable tap dancer by the name of "Peg Leg Bates" on the Ed Sullivan show. Bates had lost his leg early in life, a circumstance that would lead most people to give up any dreams of becoming a professional dancer.

But to Bates, losing a leg was not a weakness for long. He made it his strength. He put a tap at the bottom of his peg leg and developed an amazing syncopated tap-dancing style. Obviously, he stood apart from other dancers in auditions, and it wasn't long before his weakness became his strength.

Master fund-raiser Michael Bassoff has dazzled the development world by turning unappreciated staff members into great fund-raisers. He, too, likes people's weaknesses, because he knows that they can be turned into strengths. If there is a "shy" secretary in the development office he's working with, he turns that person into the staff's "best listener." Soon donors can't wait to talk to that person because she listens so well and makes people feel so important.

When Arnold Schwarzenegger became a professional actor, he had a weakness: his thick Austrian accent. It wasn't long, however, before Arnold incorporated his accent into the charm of his action-hero personality on the screen, and a former weakness became a strength. His accent became an identifying part of his character, and people everywhere began imitating it.

One of my weaknesses early in life was my difficulty in talking to people. I had no confidence in my ability to speak and converse, so I got in the habit of writing people letters and notes. After a while I got so practiced with it that I turned it into a strength. My letter writing and thank-you notes have created many relationships for me that would not have been created if I'd just focused on my shyness as a weakness.

I have four children, but I didn't begin having children until I was 35 years old. For a long time I saw myself as being "older than normal" to be a father. I worried about it. I wondered if my son or daughters would be uncomfortable with a father so old. And then I realized that this didn't have to be a weakness. I thought about who I was when I was 25, and what a difficult time I would have had being a good father back then. Soon I took this "weakness" to be a great strength.

Then one day while watching *The Little Mermaid* with my kids, I saw myself as the father in that movie— vigorous, strong, and wise, with flowing white hair. It was the perfect image. I now see my age as a major strength in raising my kids. The only "weakness" was in the way I was looking at it.

There isn't anything on your weakness list that can't be a strength for you if you think about it long enough. The problem is, our weaknesses embarrass us. But embarrassment is not real thinking. Once we really start *thinking* about our weaknesses they can become strengths, and creative possibilities emerge.

92. Try becoming the problem

Whatever type of problem you are facing, the most self-motivational exercise I know of is to immediately say to yourself, "*I* am the problem."

Because once you see yourself as the problem, you can see yourself as the solution.

This insight was dramatically described by James Belasco in *Flight of the Buffalo*.

"This is the insight I realized early and return to often," he wrote, "In most situations, I am the problem. My mentalities, my pictures, my expectations, form the biggest obstacle to my success."

By seeing ourselves as victims of our problems, we lose the power to solve them. We shut down creativity when we declare the source of the trouble to be outside of us. However, once we say, "I am the problem," there is great power that shifts from the outside to the inside. Now we can become the solution.

You can use this process the same way a detective uses a premise to clarify the crime scene. If the detective says, "What if there were two murderers, not one?" she can then think in a way that reveals new possibilities. She doesn't have to prove that there were two murderers in order to think the problem through as if there were. The same is true when you become willing always to see yourself as the problem. It is simply a way to think.

Unfortunately, our society today is in the habit of thinking the opposite of "I am the problem." *Time* magazine even ran a cover story called "A Nation of Finger Pointers," that made a powerful and persuasive case for the fact that we have become a nation of victims who "see the American dream not as striving fulfilled, but as unachieved entitlement."

In *The Six Pillars of Self-Esteem,* Nathaniel Branden writes, "To feel competent to live and worthy of happiness, I need to experience a sense of control over my existence. This requires that I be willing to take responsibility for my actions and the attainment of my goals. This means that I take responsibility for my life and my well-being."

Before I had realized the full power of a self-motivated life, I spent a lot of years pointing fingers. If I didn't have enough money, it was somebody else's fault. Even my perceived personality flaws were somebody else's fault. "I was never taught that!" I would shout in exasperation. "No one showed me early in life how to be self-sufficient!" was a complaint I voiced often.

But I was avoiding a basic truth: I was the problem. The reason I fought so hard to avoid that truth was that I never realized it contained good news. I thought it looked entirely shameful and negative. But once I discovered that accepting responsibility for the problem also gave me new power for solving it, I became free.

93. Enlarge your objective

Here is another self-motivator that also must be used as an intellectual tool only.

Take a certain goal of yours and double it. Or triple it. Or multiply it by 10. And then ask yourself, quite seriously, what you would have to do to achieve that new goal.

I used this game recently with a friend who holds a position in sales. He came to see me because he was selling $100,000 worth of product each month, the most on his team, and wanted to somehow get to $140,000.

I asked him to tell me what it would take for him to sell $200,000 worth of equipment each month. "$200,000!" he shouted. "That's impossible. I'm leading the team already with $100,000, and nobody thought that could be done."

"What would you have to do?" I persisted.

"No," he said. "You don't understand. I want to hit $140,000 a month, and even that is so hard I don't know how I'll do it."

I finally told him the theory behind this game.

If you seriously look at an outrageous goal, such as "$200,000," it will open things up for you creatively that wouldn't have opened up if you stayed looking at $140,000. He nodded slowly and reluctantly agreed to play along for a while.

"Okay," he said. "But remember, we're talking about something that's impossible."

"Fine," I said. "But if your life depended on hitting $200,000 next month, what exactly would you do?"

He laughed and then started listing things as I wrote them down on a flip pad. After he got through the ridiculous ideas, like stealing other peoples' accounts and cooking the books, he began to think of more ideas. At first it was hard.

"I'd have to be two places at once," he said. "I'd have to make twice as many presentations as I'm making. I'd have to present to two clients at once!"

Then it hit him. All of a sudden he got the idea that he might be able to stage a large presentation of his product with a number of clients in the room at one time. "I could rent a room at a hotel and have 20 people in for coffee and donuts, and I could make a big deal out of it," he said.

A number of other ideas came to him—ways to combine his cold-calling with his travel time, ways to utilize e-mail as a sales tool, how to use the administrative staff better, and ways to expand his contracts so that they would cover longer periods of time for a higher original fee, but at a lower overall rate. Idea after idea came to him while I wrote furiously on the pad.

All of the ideas were a result of his thinking big— "How would I sell $200,000 if I absolutely had to?"

He surpassed his goal of $140,000 *the very next month!*

I've often used this method for self-motivation with myself. If I have a goal of signing two seminar contracts in the next three weeks, I'll often get out a pad of paper and ask, "How would I get 10 contracts signed in three weeks?"

Inflating my goal puts me at a different level of thinking, and because I'm solving the problem of 10, I always get at least two.

If you want to really get some fresh motivational ideas, try expanding your goal. Blow it up until it scares you. Then proceed in your thinking as if it's a *must* that you achieve it. Remember that this is just a self-contained game, not a promise to anyone else. But it's a game that's fun to play because it works.

94. Give yourself flying lessons

We need heroes in our lives. They are not a sign of weakness; they are a source of strength. "Without heroes," said Bernard Malamud, "we are all plain people and we don't know how far we can go."

Heroes show us what's possible for a human being to accomplish. Therefore, heroes are very useful to anyone who is in the process of finally understanding self-motivation. But unless we consciously select our heroes in order to use them as inspiration, we simply end up *envying* great people instead of emulating them.

When used properly, a hero can be an enriching source of energy and inspiration. You don't have to have just one hero, either. Choose a number of them. Put their pictures up. Become an expert on their lives. Collect books about them.

My youngest sister, Cindy, as a shy little girl, always admired Amelia Earhardt. Not long ago, after she had reached her 30s, she revealed to me that she had been taking flying lessons. I was stunned! A few weeks after that, the family went out to a little airport outside of town to watch her fly her first solo. "I was so scared," said Cindy, "that my mouth and throat went completely dry."

Flying has nothing to do with what Cindy does for a living—she just took lessons and learned to pilot a plane because of the impression that her hero, Amelia Earhardt, made on her as a little girl.

"We grow into that which we admire," said Emmet Fox.

Before he became a famous author, Napoleon Hill was struggling as a writer and speaker. He had a friend whose restaurant business was not doing well and Hill offered to give free motivational speeches at the restaurant one night a week to help his friend increase his business. The speeches helped his friend a little, but they helped Hill a lot. He began to gain a large following.

When I read about that part of Hill's life, it gave me an idea. At the time I wanted to be a full-time speaker and I didn't know where to begin. I'd done a few seminars and talks here and there, but there was no pattern or purposeful direction to it. I decided to emulate Hill. I began putting on a free, open-to-the-public workshop every Thursday night at the company where I was working as a marketing director.

At first, the workshops were not well attended. I had to spend part of the week begging people to come. Once the audience was two people! But week by week the workshop's reputation grew and my own experience grew along with it. Soon we had large audiences waiting to get in on Thursday nights, and I credit that little free workshop with putting me into full-time public speaking.

Was it an original idea? No, I stole it. I copied a hero of mine. But our awareness of the choice involving heroes is vital for self-creation. We can envy them or we can emulate them.

The best *use* of heroes is not to just be in awe of them, but to learn something from them. To let their lives inspire us. They are only people like we are. What distinguishes them from us is the great levels they've reached in self-motivation. To passively adore them is to insult our own potential. Instead of looking *up* to our heroes, it is much more beneficial to look *into* them.

95. Hold your vision accountable

"It's not what a vision *is*," says Robert Fritz "it's what a vision *does*."

What does your vision do? Does it give you energy? Does it make you smile? Does it get you up in the morning? When you're tired, does it take you that extra mile? A vision should be judged by these criteria, the criteria of power and effectiveness. What does it *do*?

Robert Fritz is widely quoted in Peter Senge's business masterpiece, *The Fifth Discipline*. Fritz is a former musician who has taken the basic principles of creativity in music composition and applied them to creating successful professional lives. Life gets good, he argues, when we get clear on what we want to create.

Most people spend most of their waking hours trying to make problems go away. This lifelong crusade to solve one's problems is a negative and reactive existence. It sells us short and leaves us at the end of life (or at the end of the day) with, at best, the double-negative feeling of "fewer problems"!

"There is a profound difference between problem solving and creating," Fritz points out in *The Path of Least Resistance*.

"Problem solving is taking action to have something go away—the problem. Creating is taking action to have something come into being—the creation. Most of us have been raised in a tradition of problem-solving and have little real exposure to the creative process."

Step one in the creative process is having a vision of what you want to create. Without this vision, there is no way to create. Without this vision, you are only problem-eliminating, which is a double negative. It's impossible to feel positive about a life based on a double negative.

So the way to alter your thinking is to *notice* when you're drifting into, "What do I want to get rid of?" and mentally replace that thinking with, "What do I want to bring into being?"

When Fritz says that we have been "raised in a tradition" of problem solving, he is almost understating it. We are programmed and wired to think that way every day. Notice the thinking of people as they approach a challenge (even a challenge as small as an upcoming meeting with other people):

"Here's what I hope doesn't happen," one will say. "Well, here's how you can avoid that," someone else will helpfully say. "The only problem we have is this," a third person will say, attempting to make the meeting seem less frightening.

Notice that nowhere was there the question, "What would we like to *bring into being* as a result of this meeting?"

Whether the situation is as small as a meeting or as large as your whole life, the most useful question you can ask yourself is, "What do I want to bring into being?"

It's a beautiful question, because it makes no reference to problems or obstacles. It implies pure creativity. It puts you back on the positive side of life.

My friend Steve Hardison made an observation about self-motivation that I have always remembered and agreed with.

"It's just one thought," he said. "Motivational teachers repeat it many different ways, but it's just one thought: It's a binary system. Are you on or are you off?"

Are you positive or are you negative? Are you creating or are you reacting? Are you on or are you off? Are you life or are you death? Are you day or are you night? Are you in or are you out? "Is you is or is you ain't?"

And there's nothing more motivational to flip your binary switch to "on" than a clear vision of what it is that you really want. What do you want to bring into being? It doesn't matter what that vision is or how often it changes. It only matters what that vision *does*.

If your vision isn't getting you up in the morning, then make up another one. Keep at it until you develop a vision that's so colorful and clear that it puts you in action just to think about it.

96. Build your power base

Knowledge is power. What you know is your power base—it's the battery you run on. You need to charge it constantly and consciously.

Who do you want to be in charge of what you know? News directors? Radio disc jockeys? The office gossip? Tabloid newspaper editors? A pessimistic family member?

Unless we *consciously* decide to build our own knowledge base, with a sense of direction to it, then we will be programmed, totally, by random input.

Feeling miserable and alienated from life is *caused* by not being in control of what we know.

"Misery and alienation are not laid upon us by fate," wrote Colin Wilson. "They are due to the failure of the ego to accept its role as the controller of consciousness. All our experiences of happiness and intensity force the same conviction upon us, for they involve a sense of mastery."

You can be the master of your own fate. You can make choices all day long about what you are going to learn and what you are not going to learn.

"What are you reading over there?" someone may ask you. "Oh, it's just something I found in the trash," you might say.

And it might seem harmless enough to read something you found in the wastebasket because there was nothing else nearby, *but whole lives are shaped that way.* The computer term "GIGO"—garbage in, garbage out— is even truer for the human biocomputer than it is for mechanical computers.

Take control of what you know. The more you know about what motivates you, the easier it is to motivate yourself. The more you know about the human brain, the less trouble you have operating it. Knowledge is power. Respect yours and build on it.

97. Connect truth to beauty

I hate reading motivational material that thunders at me about the importance of integrity and honesty for their own sake. Somehow, that always seems to turn me off, because the writers come off like angry preachers and teachers. Hardly inspiring.

I'm always inspired better by things that are made to look interesting and fun. I'm always taken in by a promise of life being more beautiful and rarely taken in by a promise of a life being more righteous and proper.

To me, the best case to make for honesty is how beautiful it is...how clean and clear it makes the journey from current reality to the dream.

When people know *exactly* where they are, they can go somewhere from there. But being "lost" is a function of dishonesty. And when we're lost, or dishonest, anywhere we go from there is wrong. When we start with a false reading, there's no direction home.

Like Bob Dylan's rolling stone, we don't know who we are. We feel, at the core, "like a complete unknown."

Truth, on the other hand, is clear, complete, and compellingly vivid. It is solid and strong, so it can hold us steady as we climb.

"Truth," said poet John Keats, "is beauty."

The more honest we are with others and ourselves about current reality, the more energy and focus we gather. We don't have to keep track of what we told one person or what we told another.

One of the best and most positive explanations of the beauty of personal integrity was expressed by Nathaniel Branden in *The Six Pillars of Self-Esteem.* Branden, unlike most writers on the subject, sees truth and integrity as a positive part of the process of self-esteem. His point is not that we owe it to other people's sense of morality to be honest, but that we owe it to ourselves.

"One of the great self-deceptions," said Branden, "is to tell oneself, 'Only I will know.' Only I will know that I am a liar; only I will know that I deal unethically with people who trust me; only I will know that I have no intention of honoring my promise. The implication is that *my judgment is unimportant and that only the judgment of others counts.*"

Branden's writing on personal integrity is inspiring because it's directed at creating a happier and stronger self, not at a universal appeal for morality.

One of the ways we describe a work of art that is sloppy and unfinished is as "a mess." The problem with lying, or lying by omission, is that it leaves everything so incomplete—in a mess. Truth always completes the picture—any picture. And when a picture is complete, whole, and integrated, we see it as "beautiful."

I'll even hear about people—usually people who you can't believe about anything—described as "a mess." And conversely, a person who you can always count on to be honest with you is often referred to as a "beautiful" person. Truth and beauty become impossible to separate.

Truth leads you to a more confident level in your relationships with others and with yourself. It diminishes fear and increases your sense of personal mastery. Lies and half-truths will always weigh you down, whereas truth will clear up your thinking and give you the energy and clarity needed for self-motivation.

98. Read yourself a story

Abraham Lincoln used to drive his law partners to distraction. Every morning he would come into his office and read the daily newspaper *aloud* to himself. They would hear him in the next room reading in a booming voice.

Why did Lincoln do his morning reading aloud? He had discovered that he remembered and retained *twice* as much when he read aloud than when he read silently. And what he did remember, he remembered for a much longer period of time.

Perhaps it was because Lincoln was employing a second sense, the sense of hearing, and a second activity, the activity of speaking, which made his readings so memorable to him.

Any time you have an opportunity to read something that is important to you, try reading it aloud and see if you don't make twice the impression on yourself. When you discover something you want to remember, and draw upon in the future, read it aloud.

Steve Hardison, one of the most successful business consultants I have ever known, credits one origin of his success to when he was a struggling young man without money or a clue about where he wanted to go. Then one day he came across Napoleon Hill's enormous book, *Law of Success,* and read the entire volume *aloud.*

My favorite piece of writing to read aloud is Chapter 16 of Og Mandino's *The Greatest Salesman in the World.* Here's a part of it, which you may now read silently to yourself. However, if you want a real shot of adrenaline to your spirit, I recommend you mark this page and when you're alone, read it aloud like Lincoln:

"I will act now. I will act now. I will act now. Henceforth, I will repeat these words again and again, each hour, each day, every day, until the words become a habit as my breathing and the actions which follow become as instinctive as the blinking of my eyelids. With these words I can condition my mind to perform every act necessary for my success. With these words I can condition my mind to meet every challenge."

99. Laugh for no reason

Become a performer. Be an actor and a singer. Act like you already feel like you want to feel. Don't wait until the feeling motivates you. It could be a long wait.

American philosopher William James put it very clearly: "We do not sing because we are happy, we are happy because we sing."

Most of us believe an emotion, such as happiness, comes first. Then we do whatever we do, in reaction to that particular emotion. Not so, insisted James. The emotion arises simultaneously with the doing of the act. So if you want to be enthusiastic, you can get there by acting as if you were already enthusiastic. Sometimes it takes a minute. Sometimes it skips a beat. But it always works if you stay with it, no matter how ridiculous you feel doing it.

Feel ridiculous. If you want to be happy, find the happiest song you know and sing it. It works. Not always in the first few moments, but if you keep at it, it works. Just fake it until you make it. Soon your happy singing will show you how much control you do have over your own emotions.

Zen monks do a "laughing meditation" in which they all gather in a circle and get ready to laugh. At the stroke of a certain hour the teacher hits a gong, and all the monks begin to laugh. They have to laugh, whether or not they feel like it. But after a few moments the laughter becomes contagious. Soon all the monks are laughing genuinely and heartily.

Children do this, too. They start giggling for no reason (often at the dinner table or some other forbidden setting and the giggling itself makes them laugh). The truth is this: Laughter itself can make you laugh. The secret of happiness is hidden inside that last sentence.

But adults aren't always comfortable with this. Adults want kids to have *reasons* for laughing. As I used to drive my children long distances to visit relatives, I'd get most irritated when they began laughing and giggling in the back seat without reason. I developed a back-stroke swing to curb the laughter. "Why are you laughing?" I would shout. "You have no *reason* to be laughing! This is a dangerous highway and I'm trying to drive here!"

But adults, like me, might want to get back that appreciation for joyful spontaneity. We might want to confront the question, "What is the one thing that most makes me feel like singing?" And then know the answer: "Singing." What most gets you in the mood to dance? Dancing. The next time you ask someone to dance, and they say, "I don't feel like dancing," you might reply, "That's because you're not dancing."

100. Walk with love and death

"I am a coward."

That was how the book began. It was a novel I was reading not long after I had graduated from high school, and those first words staggered me. I remember staring at those words, unable to continue reading, I was so stunned. Never has a book connected with me so quickly.

For I was a coward, too. It's just that I never admitted it so openly as did the author of *A Walk with Love and Death*.

The author was Hans Konigsberger, and the book was a medieval love story later made into a movie by John Huston, but none of that mattered. What mattered was that there was another coward on the planet other than me. Even if he was fictional, the words were real enough for me.

My self-image at the time I read that book was based on my fears and nothing else. In my mind, I was truly a coward. And if someone were to tell me I'd done something brave, I'd think they were wrong somehow. Or that they didn't know how easy that thing was.

Where did this self-image come from? I don't blame my parents, because I believe we create our own pictures of ourselves, and I had a choice whether to stick with this self-image or not. (After all, I could have done what Gordon Liddy did when he was a boy—upset that he was afraid of rats, he caught some, cooked them, and ate them. Upset that he was afraid of thunder and light-ning, he strapped himself to the top of a large tree where he stayed for the duration during a major electrical storm. These kinds of things I did not do.)

Although I don't blame my parents, I can trace where I got the *idea* of my being a coward to their encouragement.

My mother, too, was afraid of everything. She lived to the age of 66 without ever having made a left hand turn in traffic, so afraid she was of oncoming traffic. (She always knew how to make a looping series of right turns to get where she was going.) She consoled me and told me that I was just like her. A coward, I thought. She was very loving and empathetic about it, but my self-image became unshakable. However, my mother said she'd try to be there to help me do the many things she knew I wouldn't be able to do.

I met my father when I was two and a half years old. He was a war hero, home from World War II, and it is reported that when he walked into our home and saw me for the first time, I looked up at his imposing uni-formed figure and said, "Who is that?"

"John Wayne," my mother should have said.

Because my father was afraid of nothing. He was a decorated soldier, a star athlete, a tough and success-ful businessman, and the list goes on. But he soon knew one thing about his little boy—no guts. And it was dis-tressing to him.

So, both parents and the child himself were all in agreement about it. The father was upset about it, the mother understood, and the boy was just scared.

That is possibly why, as I grew older, I discovered "false courage."

I discovered—through use of an intoxicating substance—that I could be who I wanted to be. But soon the marvelous discovery turned to addiction, and my life revolved around my dependency on it. They were wild times, but as anyone will tell you who's been through it, there was no growth or fulfillment during those years. They soon became an intolerable nightmare.

Fortunately, I recovered. It has been more than 20 years since I've had to resort to chemically based courage. During that recovery period, which was often difficult, I came to learn a prayer that was popular among fellow recovering people. They called it "The Serenity Prayer" and you've probably heard it. It goes like this: "God grant me the serenity to accept the things I cannot change, the courage to change the things I can and the wisdom to know the difference."

I think it was called the "serenity" prayer because that's what everyone wanted from the prayer—serenity. Abruptly ending a long period of substance abuse can leave you far short of serene. Although with each passing day it gets better and better, that prayer was something to hang on to.

But after being clean and sober started to work for me, I knew something was still missing—I knew I needed more than serenity. My deep-seated self-image of being a coward had not gone away, and so I turned my attention to the second line in the prayer, "the courage to change the things I can." In my mind, it was no longer the serenity prayer—it had become the courage prayer.

Courage was still what I lacked, and that feeling of personal cowardice was still my entire self-image. It shaped my whole "personality."

When my friend Mike Killebrew gave me Napoleon Hill's *The Master Key to Riches*, the answer to my courage prayer began to come to me. If I didn't have the courage inside of me, I would create it. And at that moment, the process of self-motivation began in earnest.

I could cite you many examples of the fears I had, but to illustrate how I overcame them, I'll use an example I referred to earlier—my fear of public speaking. I've since learned that the fear of public speaking is not unique to me. In fact, it's considered the number-one fear among our population today, even greater than the fear of death.

To me, though, it was a painful manifestation of the overall deep fear that constituted my entire personality. I laughed knowingly once when Woody Allen said that he was "afraid of the dark and feared the light of day." That was me.

When I finally made myself join an acting class to face my fear of speaking, I learned to my horror that I was the only non-actor in the class. In our first session, led by the hugely talented actress and coach Judy Rollings, I listened as everyone in the class talked about all the recent stage productions they had been in.

Judy gave us each a long monologue to learn and recite in the next session. Mine was from *Spoon River Anthology* and my character was a judge who had been mocked as a young man, but rose to judge those in the community who used to make fun of him. It was a challenging piece, and I was terrified.

I knew I had to do something harder than the recital to prepare for the recital, so I set out to do it. I memorized my part and began to perform it in front of people. I asked whoever would listen to sit down and watch me recite this piece. I did it in front of my actress friend Judy LeBeau, who had gotten me into the class. I

did it on tape and sent it to songwriter and comedian
Fred Knipe. I did it in front of my friend Kathy. I made
my children sit quietly and watch me do it over and over.
Each time, I was scared, my heart was pounding and I
hyperventilated. But each time it got easier and better.

Finally the day of the class arrived. I took the day
off from work to rehearse this little three-minute piece
all day. When class time arrived, I was extremely nervous, but not deeply panicked. In my life, there's a big
and welcome difference.

Judy Rollings asked for volunteers to perform their
monologues, and as each "experienced" actor got up to
do theirs, I gained confidence. I could see that they, too,
were very nervous. They were acting in front of peers,
which is sometimes harder than before a normal audience. They were blowing their lines and, in embarrassment, asking to start over. Some of their voices were a
little shaky. I was encouraged. Finally, with just one or
two of us left to go, I volunteered and walked slowly to
the front of the room.

What happened then is something I'll never forget.
As I went to the front of the room, just before I turned
around to face the teacher and class, a voice in my mind
spoke to me, and it said only one word: _Showtime._

With a surprising surge of energy, I delivered my
piece. My voice soared up and hit the dramatic points
and dropped down to emphasize the subtle lines and
the parts that I gave a funny interpretation to were
drawing huge laughs from the class. When I was finished, I looked back up and saw that the whole class
had burst out clapping—something Judy had told them
not to do for anybody.

When I drove home that night, I was in heaven. I
kept reciting my monologue out loud, reveling in the

memory of their laughter and clapping. The thing I thought I feared most in life was somehow mastered. And I repeated to myself the principle I had used to make it happen—the more I sweat in peacetime, the less I bleed in war.

I often look back on who I was when I first encountered the words, "I am a coward," in *A Walk With Love and Death.* And I realize that today I have something that I didn't have back then, the *knowledge that courage can be created.*

I still have fears, but I no longer *am* fear. I no longer think of myself as a coward. And when people compliment me on something I've done that they think was courageous, I don't dismiss them as being crazy or stupid.

There is a way I use to motivate myself to overcome any fear that's in my way today. It's a way I've never told anyone about until now, because it has a strange name. I call it "walk with love and death."

When I need to get through something, face something, or create a courageous action plan—I take long walks. When I walk long and far enough, a solution *always* appears. I eventually get oriented to the most creative course of action.

"When you walk," writes Andrew Weil in *Spontaneous Healing,* "the movement of your limbs is cross-patterned: the right leg and left arm move forward at the same time, then the left leg and right arm. This type of movement generates electrical activity in the brain that has a harmonizing influence on the central nervous system—a special benefit of walking that you do not necessarily get from other kinds of exercise."

I call it "a walk with love" because love and fear are opposites. (Most people think love and hate are opposites, but they are not.) The ultimate creativity occurs from a spirit of love and, as Emmet Fox says, "Love is always creative, and fear is always destructive."

I call it a "walk with death," because it is only the acceptance and awareness of my own death that gives my life the clarity that it needs to be exciting.

My walks often last a long time. Somehow, whatever challenge I'm facing appears to me from many different angles as I'm walking. I know that one of the real values is that while walking, I'm truly alone with myself—there are no phones to answer or people to talk to. I create so little of that kind of time in life, that it's always surprising how beneficial it is.

Take your own challenges out for a walk. Feel your self-motivation growing inside you, as the electricity in your brain starts to harmonize your central nervous system. You'll soon know for a fact that you have what it takes. You won't have to pray for the courage to change the things you can—you will already have it.

Afterword

101. Teach yourself the power of negative thinking

I discovered something remarkable quite by accident one night as I was conducting a workshop on goal achievement. I discovered the power of negative thinking. As the people in the workshop struggled to list their goals on a piece of paper, I ran out of patience.

"How will you get what you want if you don't know what it is?" I asked the room, half of which still had empty sheets of paper and empty facial expressions.

"Okay," I said, "Let's put these goals away. I want to try something different. Take out a new sheet of paper and do this. Write down what you *don't want* in your life. List every major problem and source of discomfort you have. All your worries. All the negative things you can think of, even if they haven't come into reality yet. Even if they are just things you don't want to happen in the future. Take your time and be thorough."

What I saw happen next startled me. The entire room's energy level picked up, and everyone in the workshop was writing and writing and writing. It wasn't long before some people asked if they could use a second page.

Something strange and electric was filling the air as people aired their fears and grievances. Pages were flooded with ink, and hands and fingers had to be shaken out so people wouldn't cramp up from writing so much. When I called an end to the exercise, the room was buzzing.

I had obviously let something loose that wasn't there before. At that moment I got my first true look at the power of the negative. Actually, I had seen it before. When I took the time to look back over my life, I realized that saying *no* was always a stronger stand to take than saying *yes*. Saying *no* is drawing a line in the sand. It is taking a stand. It is putting your foot down. It is passionate. It is powerful. Compared to saying *no*, saying *yes* is wobbly and wishy-washy. I said *yes* to a thousand drinks of alcohol in my life. But it wasn't until one hung-over suicidal morning when I said *no* that my life got completely turned around. When the cave man drew the line in the dirt outside his cave and said no to the saber-tooth tiger, his family was finally safe.

Saying *no* is powerful, because it comes from the deepest part of the soul. There are some things we just won't tolerate.

Once we fully understand the power of those *no's* deep inside of us, we can use them to motivate ourselves like never before.

In the workshop I was telling you about, once the people filled their papers up with what they *didn't* want, we got busy converting problems into goals. You don't want to go bankrupt? Then let's get a prosperity plan going! You don't want to weigh as much as your two best friends combined? Then let's get a nutrition and exercise program going! Any *no* can be converted to a powerful *yes*.

So if you're stuck without any truly motivating goals, dreams or commitments, then go negative first. Figure out what you absolutely don't want—what you absolutely fear and dread and refuse to let in to your life—then convert it to its opposite, positive form and see what happens. You'll be more motivated than you ever dreamed you could be.

I have used this in one-on-one meetings with people who wouldn't open up and tell me what they wanted. I simply asked them to tell me what they *didn't* want to have happen and we were off to the races. Once you know what that is, you can convert the conversation to exciting plans and objectives. This explains why so many successful people had difficult upbringings, sometimes living in the harshest poverty. They connected very early to what they didn't want. The rest was clear sailing.

The next time you lack passion when thinking of what you want, try turning it around. Ask yourself what you absolutely don't want, and then feel the energy building in you to overcome that problem.

That energy you're feeling is the deepest and most primal form of motivation.

Index

About the
Author

Steve Chandler is a sales trainer and a keynote and convention speaker who lives and works in Phoenix, Arizona.

He has brought his workshops and seminars to over 400 different companies including Motorola, Texas Instruments, IBM and Intel.

His previous bestselling motivational books include *100 Ways to Motivate Yourself, Reinventing Yourself, 50 Ways to Create Great Relationships,* and *17 Lies that are Holding You Back and the Truth That Will Set You Free.*

Chandler is often a guest speaker and coach in the TopTHINK Strategic Quest Travel Adventure series (910-485-6944) and can also be reached at 100Ways@Compuserve.com.